MURDER
OF A
MAFIA
DAUGHTER

ALSO BY CATHY SCOTT:

The Killing of Tupac Shakur

The Murder of Biggie Smalls

Death in the Desert: The Ted Binion Homicide Case

Seraphim Rose: The True Story and Private Letters

MURDER OF A MAFIA DAUGHTER

The Life and Tragic Death of Susan Berman

CATHY SCOTT

Fort Lee, New Jersey

For Susan

Published by Barricade Books Inc.
185 Bridge Plaza North, Suite 308-A
Fort Lee, NJ 07024
www.barricadebooks.com

Library of Congress Cataloging-in-Publication Data
Scott, Cathy.
  Murder of a Mafia daughter : the life and tragic death of
  Susan Berman / Cathy Scott.
     p. cm.
  Includes bibliographical references.
  ISBN 1-56980-238-6 (casebound)
  1. Berman, Susan, 1945–2000. 2. Murder victims--Nevada--
  Biography. I. Title.

HV6533.N215 S38 2002
364.15'23'092--dc21
[B]   2002026063

First Printing
Manufactured in Canada

Contents

Acknowledgments

There are many to thank.

Much kudos to Barricade Books for believing in the project, and especially editor Allan J. Wilson and Jeff Nordstedt for their gentle guidance.

To my agent, Frank Weimann, CEO and president of The Literary Group in New York City, for landing me the contract.

To Los Angeles agent Mickey Freiberg for his attaboys.

To my writer friends—Susan Gembrowski, Lora Shaner, Myram Borders, Frank Alexander, Kevin Powell, Charlene "Charlie" Fern, Kae Reed, Vickie Pynchon, John L. Smith, Larry Henry, Andy Rathbone, Randy Dotinga, Matt O'Brien, and Gary C. King—for their collective understanding of what it takes to put pen to paper.

This book would not have been complete but for those who generously agreed to be interviewed so that their friend's story would be accurate. My warm thanks to Danny Goldberg, Guy Rocha, Ruthie Bartnof, Ed Bayley, Julie Smith, Elizabeth Mehren, Lou DeCosta, Harvey Myman, Dick Odessky, Hal Rothman, David Millman, Bob Miller, Oscar Goodman, Rilo Weisner, Kevin McPherson,

Gilberta Najamy, and Deke Castleman for their insightful recollections into the real Susan, and particularly Stephen M. Silverman—he knows what his role was with this project and for that I am grateful; to Sandy Mallin and Adele Barantz for their history lessons on Las Vegas Temple Beth Shalom; and private investigator Bobbi Bacha with Blue Moon Investigations for her expertise.

To the men and women in uniform at the Los Angeles and Galveston police departments, in particular LAPD Lieutenant Clay Farrell, and the L.A. and Westchester county prosecutors' offices, for their help in pointing me in the right direction; the Clark County Library; and the Special Collections office at the University of Nevada-Las Vegas.

In addition to those who helped directly, I salute my colleagues in the press whose articles provided background information, in particular the *New York Times, Los Angeles Times, New York Post, Galveston County Daily News, Texas Monthly*, and *New York* magazine. I should also mention the television specials, including those that appeared on Fox's "America's Most Wanted," "ABC News," and "Prime Time Live."

And, as always, to my family for believing in me, especially: My mother and fellow writer Eileen Rose Busby; my twin sister Cordelia Mendoza and her husband Bob; my big brother Dr. J. Michael Scott and his wife Sharon; my other big brother Jon Scott and his wife Loretta; my stepmother Helen Scott; my son Raymond Somers Jr. (who is the stalwart

Web master for www.cathyscott.com) and my daughter-in-law Karen; and my grandkids Claire and Jake. I don't know what I'd do without any of them.

Thanks to my hiking and dog park friends, particularly Eva Wardlaw, Tamera Burton, CJ Boisvert, Brenda Dreissigacker, Denise Meeker, and Patty Barnes—those days and evenings helped me get through it.

And thanks also to my late father, James Melvin Scott (who proudly published his memoir *The Missouri Kid*) for his erstwhile encouragement until his December 2001 death. Did I thank him enough while he was here? Probably not. If he's listening, I thank him now, with all my heart.

Prologue

THIS IS A STORY that begins in old Las Vegas with gangsters and the boys from the Jewish mob. It moves to New York City and the *literati* and ends in Beverly Hills with the glitterati. It's a story about a path to murder.

The slaying of Susan Berman in the winter of 2000 had all the earmarks of a professional hit aimed at a person born into the Mafia. Or is that just how the killer intended it to appear, to lead investigators to the assumption that it was a mob hit? Was it someone else who wanted her dead? If it was not a mob hit, then who else could have done it? And why? These are the questions I pursued for the many months as I covered Susan Berman's murder, looking for clues.

In my research for this story, I've gotten to know Susan. I drove the route from her Las Vegas home to her Benedict Canyon house in Beverly Hills. I visited the restaurants she frequented in the town she loved and called home for the last 17 years of her life. I walked through the Las Vegas house on South Sixth Street where she lived for the first 13 years of her life. It was a bright, cheerful house. I imagined her as a child, running down the long hallway into the arms of the father she adored.

I went to the University of California at Berkeley campus where Susan got her master's degree and where protests against the war in Vietnam were rampant. Susan made lifelong friends while attending Berkeley—friends in the writing world who later tossed work her way.

I visited her home in Benedict Canyon where she was murdered, and found it gloomy and dark. Someone else lives there now.

I visited the cemetery in East Los Angeles where Susan was entombed alongside her mother, father, and uncle. A recent visitor left flowers in bud vases for her mother Gladys, father Davie, and uncle Chickie. Susan's vases, one on either side of her shiny-brass headstone, were empty. I stood there looking at her grave, regretting I hadn't brought her a flower.

I only wish I could have met Susan face to face. She wanted so much to be famous, to be recognized for her work. Today, after her death, her work has become well known. It has left its mark on Las Vegas. Susan's name and books have been the subject of scores of news reports. There's a long waiting list at public libraries to check out her writings. The books sell for high prices, in the hundred range, on Internet auction sites. Had she lived to see it, Susan would have been pleased. She no doubt would have chuckled at the irony of it. She also would have pondered the intrigue of her own murder investigation as it unfolded. It was her forte, titillating clues pursued with a vengeance. All evidence points to Susan being cut down by someone she not only knew, but who was a trusted and beloved friend. That irony, too, however tragic, would have piqued Susan's interest.

This is her story.

Chapter 1
Murder of a
Mafia Daughter

IT WAS THE morning of December 23, 2000, a Saturday and the last weekend before Christmas. Marvin Karp was up before 7:30 AM. He heard barking. When he looked out his front window, he saw two small dogs in his front yard. One was dragging a leash behind him.

Many people in Beverly Hills have dogs who bark. But the barking this time was so excited and so prolonged that some residents noticed the commotion. Marvin Karp was startled enough to check it out.

The dogs belonged to Susan Berman, Karp's next-door neighbor. "Those dogs were *always* barking," he said.

That's it, Karp thought to himself as he looked out at the noisy dogs. "I was ready to go over there [to Susan's] and ask her, 'Hey, why are your dogs loose?' I didn't know her very well, so I didn't," he said.

About 30 hours later, Karp learned why the dogs were out.

The neighbors on the other side of Susan also thought it strange when Susan's third dog ran to their house. It was odd that her dogs were outside on their own, especially since Susan treated them like they were her children, and because she was in a lease dispute, in part, because of the noisy canines.

The next morning, Sunday, December 24, the dogs were still loose. Marvin Karp went outside, but he didn't see any activity at Susan's house. He walked past Susan's to the neighbors' house on the other side to see if they knew anything. The neighbors had already been in Susan's yard, they told him, and saw that her side gate was open and the back door ajar. They were alarmed. "Nobody wanted to go in there," Marvin said. "It looked suspicious." The neighbors, by this time worried, called police to investigate.

For a couple of Susan Berman's friends, the day before Christmas was a happy time, in anticipation of an annual get-together. But instead of gathering with friends for the holidays, as Susan had planned to do and as she had done every year before, police, investigators, and crime-scene analysts swarmed her modest bungalow in Benedict Canyon, just above the city of Beverly Hills.

Susan had also scheduled a dinner that Saturday night with her cousin Deni Marcus. When Susan didn't show, those close to her began calling each other. After learning the tragic news, Susan's friends gathered at her house.

Instead, Christmas Eve marked the day the lifeless body of Berman, born to a Las Vegas mobster in 1945, was found in her home. Her three precious wirehaired fox terriers—Lulu, Romeo, and Golda (named after former Israel Prime Minister Golda Meir)—were running inside and out, barking frantically.

Their owner, Susan Jane Berman, 55 years old, had been murdered with a single gunshot to the back of her head at close range, Chicago mob-style.

Susan's father had always protected her as a child, even whisking her away from Las Vegas and mob unrest for Los Angeles getaways, and heightening the windows of her bedroom to prevent an abduction.

Davie Berman wasn't there to protect his precious Susie this time. She was all alone.

The wooded Benedict Canyon has a storied past. It is home to many Hollywood stars. It also is where actress Sharon Tate was murdered. That grisly slaying happened in the summer of 1969 in her rented house on Cielo Drive, less than a half mile from where Susan Berman rented a home nearly three decades later. Tate, eight months pregnant with director Roman Polanski's child, had been brutally murdered by strangers—deranged members of the Manson Family. Conversely, police believed Berman was taken by surprise and killed by someone she knew—perhaps someone she knew too well.

In 1838 a Spanish land grant was assigned to El Rancho Rodeo de las Aguas (translated, it means The Ranch of the Gathering Waters), named for the streams that emptied into the area from out of the canyons above, including Canada de los Encinos, or

Glen of the Green Oaks, now known as Benedict Canyon. After oil exploration in the area in 1906 failed to pan out, Burton E. Green formed Rodeo Land and Water Company to develop the parcel. The next year, Green opened luxurious, curving, tree-lined streets in the subdivision of Beverly Hills, so named in honor of President Taft's Massachusetts vacation hideaway. In 1911, Beverly Gardens Park was established, with fourteen lavishly planted neighborhood blocks backdropped by the canyons slicing into the Santa Monica Mountains above. Then, in 1914, P.E. Benedict allowed holdings in Benedict, Franklin, and Higgins canyons to be included as parts of the community.

Thus, the Ranch of the Gathering Waters was incorporated and the city of Beverly Hills, 90210, was born. Benedict Canyon Drive, a couple of miles from downtown Beverly Hills, intersects with the famous Sunset Strip near the landmark Beverly Hills Hotel. Celebrities' homes dot the winding, narrow canyon road.

Beverly Hills is a small town for the wealthy with luxury homes and shops within just six square miles where mostly the more fortunate live in comfort. Its first mayor was actor Will Rogers. The city has no billboards or industry. There is no hospital or cemetery to remind residents of their eventual mortality. It's been said that "no one is born or dies in Beverly Hills."

Susan enjoyed the prestige of living among the upper crust, especially in Benedict Canyon. She looked at it as her birthright. And she felt safer there than anywhere else she had ever lived—and Susan resided, at one time or another, on each coast—although she never really felt 100-percent safe anywhere.

She lived her life with caution, almost as a recluse, in her run-down Beverly Hills home, surrounded by wealth—which she was born into but which eluded her most of her adult years. She wrote, in her 1981 memoir *Easy Street: The True Story of a Mob Family*: "There are scars within me that will probably never heal; I have uncontrollable anxiety attacks that occur without warning; I am never secure and live with a dread that apocalyptic events could happen at any moment. I am never settled but prefer instead to live a rather nomadic existence without much furniture or possessions. Death and love seem linked forever in my fantasies and the *Kaddish* will ring always in my ears."

Benedict Canyon is where Susan Berman was killed by an intruder December 22, 2000, the Friday before Christmas.

Susan's more-than-modest wood-shingled rented bungalow sat on the busy canyon road. The area was wooded and green. Susan's house was in disrepair at the time of her death. She blamed her landlady. She had very few belongings, mostly mementos. One was a long, gold key chain, given to Susan's father by a Denver gangster. The inscription read, "DB from Ray Ryan, 1949." Susan used it until her death. She didn't own real property; her most expensive possessions were a used SUV and a desktop computer, which her friends later described as her "precious computer," her lifeline to freelance work. Most of her friends shuttled her to and from vet and doctor appointments, the movies, restaurants, and the supermarket. She enjoyed the company, preferring not to drive herself; her car was out of commission most of the time anyway. And Susan was paranoid about driving, especially over bridges.

Her home was directly next to heavy traffic. Susan had lived in the same house, at 1527 Benedict Canyon Drive, years earlier in better times. When a bullet was fired from a handgun inside her home, no one but the shooter—and Susan's dogs—heard it. The killer walked out of Susan's house and into the night completely undetected.

Even though Susan was Jewish, each year she'd spend Christmas day with one of her closest friends, Susie Amateau Harmon, a friend since they boarded together at the preparatory Chadwick School in Los Angeles. Susie Harmon lived in Arizona, but each year Susan joined her at Harmon's mother's L.A. home. The family once again was expecting Susan for Christmas dinner. She told them she planned to bring her friend and personal manager Nyle Brenner.

Susan no longer had family of her own. They all were dead, except for a couple of cousins. Her closest friends, and her cousins, had become her immediate family. She depended on them for moral support. And, more times than not over the years, for financial backing too. Susan made a point of surrounding herself with successful people, those with clout in the entertainment, music, and literary worlds, people she knew she could turn to in a bind.

That Friday night, December 22, Susan had an unexpected late-night guest. Police believed it was a friend who appeared unannounced, one who ended up killing her. Susan had been working on her computer at home. Earlier in the day, she had made the usual lengthy phone calls to friends. Nothing she said alarmed anyone. And she didn't mention she was expecting company. It was a typical winter day in the Los Angeles basin: no rain, mostly clear, with a few scattered clouds, and the temperature reaching 63 degrees, considered a pleasant December day for southern California.

Earlier that evening, Susan had gone to an early dinner and movie with comedy writer Rich Markey. Using their Writers Guild passes, they saw *Best in Show*, a dog-show comedy. Susan was upbeat, talking over dinner about her latest book proposal and an agent's interest in it. After she got home, because the temperature had dropped and there was a chill in her old house, Susan put on her favorite sweatpants and T-shirt.

Police surmised that Susan's intruder had arrived sometime that night, with the shelter of darkness protecting him from being seen.

Susan's neighbors became alarmed a day and a half later, on December 24, when her three dogs were still running loose, a day after they first spotted them outside. When the neighbors picked up the phone and called the Los Angeles Police Department, it was just before 12:30 in the afternoon. A dispatch operator radioed it out as a routine possible intruder call.

Responding patrol officers arrived a few minutes later at Susan's home. A uniformed officer knocked on her door, but no one answered. He tried the handle on the front door. It was unlocked. He opened it and called out. There was no response. The house was quiet. Another officer walked to the side gate, next to the unattached single-car garage, and into the backyard. There, he saw that Susan's back door was ajar. Both officers, with their sidearms drawn, slowly went inside the house. They found Susan's body laying on her spare-room floor, face down. The officers immediately radioed for paramedics and a crime-scene team. They secured the home and cordoned the yard and house with yellow police tape while they waited for backup.

Drivers, usually in a hurry speeding along the country-like meandering road, slowed to a crawl to see what was happening.

Within minutes, an ambulance and fire truck arrived. Susan's body lay on the spare-room floor. Paramedics checked her body for a pulse. There was none. Her body was rigid and cold to the touch. Her head and hair were covered in dried blood. There was no need to take her to a hospital; she'd expired a day or two earlier. Paramedics pronounced her dead at 1:20 PM, about 40 minutes after neighbors dialed 911.

Two of Susan's dogs darted back and forth into the room as paramedics worked. An LAPD officer, one of the first on the scene, caught the small dogs and put them in his patrol car. The third dog was at a neighbor's.

A few minutes later, the first member of the investigative team arrived, then the second. They were detectives Brad Roberts and Ronald Phillips, on call and dispatched to the house that holiday afternoon.

The detectives were briefed by the uniformed officers who were first on the scene. The two officers stepped aside and let the investigators take the lead, per protocol in investigations.

Susan's bullet wound in the back of her head was from a 9-millimeter pistol. Later, a Las Vegas mob attorney called it a "Chicago mob-style hit." But that didn't mean it was executed by the mob, he pointed out. Investigators, too, felt it looked staged, like the killer had wanted it to appear like a mob hit to steer police away from the *real killer* and his motives.

Police quickly surmised that Susan had either been surprised by an assailant or had known her killer, most probably a man. It was unlike the careful and cautious Susan to leave her house unlocked, let alone a door wide open. Officers followed bloody paw prints from Susan's dogs to the spare bedroom, where Susan's body was on the cold hardwood floor. At first, police said she'd been dead for a day, maybe more. Near her body was a lock of her long, dark hair next to a pool of dried blood. Her friends often teased her that she'd kept the same dated style, always with bangs and very much a 1960s 'do, since her girlhood days. It was almost a Cleopatra hair cut: long, straight, near-black hair with flat perfectly cut bangs. Like her mother, she kept it long, shiny, and black. In college, Susan's hair was waist-length.

Later in the day, when a few stunned friends made their way to Susan's home, the sight of the grisly but spartan murder scene left them numb. There was nothing valuable in her house, nothing to be stolen. Lieutenant Clay Farrell, the lead LAPD Robbery-Homicide investigator on the Berman case, commented, "Her house was sad. It was barren. Let me put it this way, you wouldn't want to live there."

Her friend Ruthie Bartnof said it was just another side to the complicated Susan. "I don't know why she chose to live such a spartan life," Bartnof said. "It was always like that."

It was surprising to officers that Susan had enjoyed such a rich and lavish childhood only to die a pauper, with nothing of value in her name except copyrights to her out-of-print books. She had no assets. In fact, she owed most of her friends money.

Susan had nothing of value to leave anyone. Still, she had written it down in a will.

Julie Smith, a mystery writer and one of Susan's closest friends, was executor of Susan's will.

"Susan had three wills," Julie said. "The last one was the one in force." Ainsley Prior, also a close friend to Susan, commented, "She had made certain provisions in her will, including a home for her fox terriers. Police had taken the two dogs to the local humane society. Lulu went to Susan's next-door neighbors. The other two went to a sanctuary, living on a ranch for fox terriers." Ainsley visited the two in the sanctuary and told Susan's friends that she had never seen them happier.

Susan also included her college friend Bobby Durst in her will. To him, she bequeathed her prized silver medallion that was once her father's, given to him by her aunt Lillian. Susan had nothing else of value and no cash. Her book royalties had either ended or trickled down to barely nothing as the titles, one by one, went out-of-print.

On January 2, 2001, a Tuesday, Susan's friends buried her in a huge mausoleum at the Home of Peace cemetery on Whittier Boulevard in Boyle Heights in East Los Angeles, formerly a Jewish community, now a *barrio*. Just one Jewish-owned family business remained in the nearby retail area that was once a community hub. Susan's funeral was held earlier at the Hillside Memorial Park, at 6001 Centinela Avenue in Culver City, which is owned by Temple Israel of Hollywood, where Susan was a member. After a few cloudy days, the sun was out, as if it were especially meant for Susan. She was dressed in a long black velvet dress with white trim that had belonged to the grandmother of Sareb and Mella Kaufman, her ex-boyfriend's children whom she raised as her own. A mortuary van then took Susan's body to the Home of Peace Memorial Park. Her casket was placed in a crypt at the end of a wall inside the mausoleum, in the Eternal Life corridor, next to her parents and her Uncle Chickie. At long last, Susan was home again, with her family.

"Fortunately, [Susan's vault] is on the second level," her friend Kim Lankford, an actor who played Ginger Ward on "Knot's Landing," told a reporter. "And there's nobody on the other side to annoy her." Those gathered sang "On the Sunny Side of the Street," written by Dorothy Fields and Jimmy McHugh. Susan and her father's favorite lyrics were, "If I never had a cent/I'd be rich as Rockefeller/Gold dust at my feet/On the sunny side of the street." Susan's father had taught her how to play the song on the family's piano.

Susan's treasured photos of friends and family were placed inside her casket, with her.

"We put all her favorite people in there," Kim Lankford noted. "Couldn't fit everybody in."

Many of Susan's friends knew of each other, but had never met, although they felt as if they'd known each other for years, because Susan so often spoke about them all. They were a loyal group of friends. After Susan's death, they got to know each other better. They had a common bond: To help police bring Susan's killer to justice.

Sareb Kaufman, Susan's surrogate son, organized a memorial service for Susan the first week in February at the Writers Guild of America's headquarters on West Third Street in Los Angeles.

Conspicuously absent from both the funeral and memorial services was Susan's longtime friend Bobby Durst. That fact did not go unnoticed. Susan's friends found it curious, but that was about it. Investigators found it noteworthy, especially since Sareb had gone to great lengths to make sure the media were not informed in advance, so Durst wouldn't be inundated by flashing lights and microphones in his face. Still, Bobby stayed away.

Not long after Susan's death, Sareb told a reporter, "Susan loved mysteries. She even wrote a few. She would have loved this one." He and her closest friends pointed out that she would have been miffed at the circumstances surrounding her own death, and would have loved to stick around to find out the ending. Susan's life—and even her death—was colorful. It was always that way, starting from birth.

Chapter 2
Poor Little Rich Girl

Whatever I am now, and whatever I become, I will always be, first and foremost, Davie and Gladys Berman's only child.

—Susan Berman
from *Easy Street*

"I LIVED IN Las Vegas, the center of the world, and my dad owned it," Susan Berman wrote in *Lady Las Vegas: The Inside Story Behind America's Neon Oasis.* "My strange Vegas pedigree allowed me to be raised in wealth and glamour by a man who owned the town...."

Hers was a childhood of luxury, with mobster bodyguards acting as playmates and a full-time housekeeper and cook acting as a mother in a comfortable, opulent setting. It was the 1950s in a well-to-do downtown Las Vegas neighborhood. Susan was lavished with gifts and spoiled by her father, Davie Berman, an underworld Las Vegas operative. The family didn't exactly know what Davie did for a living, only that he worked at casinos and appeared to be in a high position. Whatever it was, Susan's mother, Gladys Betty Berman, knew it was dangerous. It threw her into periods of deep depression and seclusion. The same would happen to her daughter in her adult years.

Susan Jane Berman was born in Minneapolis, Minnesota, on May 18, 1945, a Friday. Two months later, in July 1945, Susan's life in Las Vegas began when her mother took her from the Tri Cities to southern Nevada by train, aboard a Union Pacific coach car. Her father had gone to Las Vegas months earlier to prepare for his family's relocation to the desert. The town had a population of just 16,000 back then and was on the brink of becoming a gambling boomtown.

The Bermans moved into the El Rancho Vegas, in a bungalow, the only place where hotel owners could get a war-rationed telephone installed. It was the original luxurious hotel-casino in the desert outside town, a landscaped and waterfalled resort complex covering 66 acres. It was on U.S. Highway 91, which later became known as the Los Angeles Highway, and, ultimately, the Las Vegas Strip.

The Bermans stayed at the El Rancho for several months until Susan's mother found a quaint and comfortable house downtown, at 721 South Sixth Street. Susan would spend the first 13 years of her life in that house. Later, Susan's parents went to the pound and got her a dog they named Blackie.

Their home was a cozy two-bedroom, two-bath, tan stucco single-story English tudor with a dining room, large living room, two-sink front bathroom, a large brick fireplace, cedar-lined closets, air conditioning—a real luxury in those days; other people, if they were lucky, had swamp coolers—and trees in both the front and back yards. At the back of the lot, Davie had workers build a large custom playhouse for Susie about the size of the single-car garage.

It was a comfortable home and became a meeting place for Davie and his partners. They spent their time either in the dining room—the first room they walked into off the kitchen—or in the living room.

By Las Vegas standards in the 1940s, the downtown neighborhood was considered upper-class. The Berman house sat on one-sixteenth of an acre and was built in 1937, one of the earliest houses in Las Vegas, and listed as parcel number 139-34-410-212 with the Clark County tax assessor's office. Davie paid $7,000 in cash for the home, but ultimately spent nearly $8,000 in renovations and improvements, for a total investment of $15,000 (in 1983, the last time the house sold, it went for $105,000). At one point, the home was included in a book of landmark houses because it was one of the few English tudors in the area.

Susan's father summoned a contractor to move the windows of the bedrooms, including Susan's, high off the ground so kidnappers could not grab her. (Her father's phobia carried over into Susan's adult years, when she was afraid to stand next to a window in a high-rise building.) The height was also intended to prevent a drive-by shooting during mob unrest. Davie had the second bathroom added, with full-length mirrors on the bathroom doors, and huge cedar-lined closets in the bedrooms and in the hallway. A hotel gardner planted grass and stucco birdbaths were added.

Susan grew up riding horses from a livery stable on Fifth Street, next door to the Last Frontier hotel and loped across the desert in western togs from Smith and Chandler. Or her parents took her out on Lake Mead in the hotel's boat. She walked with her bodyguard Lou Raskin to Cliff's market, the corner grocery just two blocks away. She played cards, swam in the Flamingo's pool, retrieving dimes from the pool bottom, and counted money with her father in the casino counting room. Weekend outings included the Del Mar Race Track where "the turf meets the surf" in north San Diego County. The Bermans had box seats near Harry James and Betty Grable, who each owned thoroughbred horses.

Every night, Susan's father rushed home from the casino so he could read his daughter a bedtime story, then returned to work. He gave her a casino house account when she was just seven so she could go to a vacant room and order shrimp cocktails from room service. He commissioned a portrait of her in pigtails that hung in the lobby of the Flamingo. Susan was a tomboy. In *Lady Las Vegas*, she described herself as a girl who was "short and scruffy" and "wore jeans, a Western shirt, and cowboy boots; my knees were always skinned, my nose was sunburned from living in the Flamingo Hotel pool."

When Susan was nine, her parents took her on a

five-day trip to New York City. They were met with a limousine and stayed at the Hampshire Hotel on West 47th Street in the heart of Midtown Manhattan in the theatre district. They took in two Broadway shows, *Guys and Dolls* and *Wish You Were Here*. They went to Rumplemayer's on Central Park South for a Continental cuisine breakfast, then shopped at Fifth Avenue's F.A.O. Schwartz where Susan's father bought her an expensive toy switchboard. Susan fell in love with the city.

It was an unusual childhood, and a spoiled one.

Young Susie Berman lived in a world of privilege: the best schools, outings to Los Angeles and the best restaurants, and the best star entertainment the Las Vegas Strip had to offer. She was lavished with expensive toys and gifts from high rollers and famous clientele and possessed a name that accorded her deference in high society. Susan was born into Mafia royalty. Her father was, as she once wrote, "one of the founders of the Syndicate, a trusted partner of Meyer Lansky, Frank Costello, and Bugsy Siegel."

Susan loved her childhood, but didn't realize at the time just how lucky she was. "The life [my father] gave my mother and me was glamourous, but it seemed ordinary to me," she wrote in *Lady Las Vegas*. "I lived with them, my dog Blackie, and intermittent middle-aged Jewish bodyguards my father referred to as 'best friends.'"

During an interview for A&E network's *The Real Las Vegas: The Inside Story Behind America's Neon*

Oasis, a documentary series Susan co-wrote and co-produced, she said, "There was an ebullience and exhilaration in the late 1940s and '50s. You were coming to Vegas. I knew everyone, and my dad owned it. You were coming to the center of the world, and it was terribly exciting."

Susan's mother, however, didn't feel the same as Susan about her desert home. She became depressed and felt isolated. Susan's father sent his wife three times a week to Los Angeles for treatment, which included shock treatments that left her mother unresponsive and reserved. When Susan was 10, her mother had gotten better and she moved with her to an apartment in Westwood, California, so her mother could undergo therapy nearby. For the fifth grade, Susan started classes at the Fairburn Elementary School on Overland Avenue. Her bodyguard Lou, who stayed with them in L.A., continued to walk Susan to and from school. In the summer Susan returned to Las Vegas to be with her father. Her mother stayed behind to continue her treatments.

Susan's father would get her together with kids from the casino. One childhood acquaintance was Bob Miller—Susan called him Bobby—who would go on to become a two-term Nevada governor. His father worked at the Riviera Hotel. It was in 1955 that Miller met Susan, shortly after Miller's family moved to the desert. His father was Ross Miller, a Chicago bookmaker said to be associated with the Outfit, who, with Davie Berman, ran the Riviera, which opened April 19, 1955. Twelve years later, in 1967, Riviera executives, including Ross, were indicted for skimming from the casino for the mob.

"We were young children together," Bob Miller said. "Our fathers were partners for a short while, in the 1950s. We were thrown together, as children, when our fathers would bring us to the casino and we'd see each other. I remembered her father. I remembered his face. I knew that he was partners with my dad. I honestly, unfortunately, didn't get to know her as well as I would have liked to."

Susan recalled, in her book *Easy Street,* the get-togethers: "Every day, no matter what, my mother took me, in my early years, to the Flamingo pool, and then to the Riviera pool.... All the kids of the owners swam and dove in that long, blue pool all summer."

Susan contacted Miller while she worked on a TV special. It was the first time they'd spoken since they were kids. "She did a telephonic interview of me [for an A&E documentary]," he said, "then sent a TV crew to interview me."

In her book, *Lady Las Vegas*, Susan described Miller. "He's Governor now," she wrote. "When I knew him he was tall, gangly Bobby Miller, my dad's partner Ross Miller's kid.... I didn't know Bobby well but I remember that he was a lifeguard by the pool and hung around the massage-parlor part of Mike Tulane's Health Club on the sixth floor of the Riv, with all the other owners' sons, hoping to get a glimpse of a showgirl coming out.

"Most people love him in town. They say he is totally committed to Las Vegas and will probably be a senator." After two terms as governor, however, Miller returned to practicing law in Las Vegas.

Susan often wrote about, and said in interviews, that her father started the first Jewish temple in Las Vegas so she could go to Sunday school and "the wiseguys would have a place to worship." The *shul* they attended was the Las Vegas Jewish Community Center, at 13th Street and Carson Avenue, seven blocks from the Berman home.

"He built it for me," Susan would say. Susan once wrote that her father was "a Jewish role model" and "extremely proud of being Jewish. He felt that for a Jewish child to be properly brought up, there must be a synagogue, a rabbi, and a cantor in evidence."

In fact, it was a group of 25 families who founded the temple. If Davie Berman was involved, no one alive today remembers. "As far as I remember while I was on the board, he had nothing to do with it," said original board member Charles Salton. "I knew who he was. He was one of the boys on the Strip. But he didn't have anything to do with starting the Temple."

In 1931, a group of people began worshiping behind a store, explained Sandy Mallin, past president of the board of directors of Temple Beth Shalom. "In the early '40s, they met in the rectory of the Catholic Church downtown at Bridger and Second Street," Mallin said. "In 1944 and 1945, they began raising money for a temple. In 1946, the temple opened at 13th Street and Carson Avenue." It was Las Vegas's first Jewish temple and the second in the state, Mallin said.

Las Vegan Adele Baratz also remembered how the temple got started. "The Bermans came to town after the temple was organized," she said. "So did Hank Greenspun [publisher of the *Las Vegas Sun*]. They all were members. The original people who were behind it, Nate Mack, Harry Mack, and Louie Mack, got it off the ground. Davie Berman may have attended temple, but he wasn't a founder. He could have given money. The way it got started was that the Macks decided they wanted a temple. They went around to the Jewish people who lived here, in the 1940s. They asked if they would pledge so much, but [the founders] didn't want it right away. As soon as they started building the temple, they collected on the pledges. This was at 13th Street and Carson, around 1945. It was called the Las Vegas Jewish Community Center. When it moved to Oakey, in 1956, it was called Temple Beth Shalom. My brother, Charles Salton, is the oldest living member of the Temple. I don't think there's anybody else here who's been a member since it started. Most Jewish people who moved to the town went to the temple to meet people. It started out as the Sons and Daughters of Israel. They'd have parties for some of the holidays."

After the temple moved to the Oakey location, Susan wrote in *Lady Las Vegas*, her father took her to the Friday night services.

Temple Beth Shalom moved in 1999 to Summerlin, a planned community in northwest Las Vegas, after selling its Oakey location to a Christian Church.

Ruthie Bartnof, a former Las Vegan and a close friend to Susan, said it was her understanding that Davie contributed money for the synagogue, quietly and behind the scenes. After Susan's murder and Ruthie's son's death six months later, Ruthie had a plaque installed for them at Temple Beth Shalom's new location.

"I went to the temple and put a plaque up in their names," Ruthie said. "That was their home-town. Davie was one of the founders. All those casi-no people contributed big money. Susan went to temple with me in Los Angeles. She followed the Jewish laws. Her mother wasn't Jewish, but her father was. I think it brought her closer to him."

Susan's first-class life in the desert opulence abruptly ended when her father died in 1957, then her mother the following year. In 1959, the home in which Susan had experienced so much happiness was sold to a man named Ellis Johnson and his wife Alline (today the house serves as a law office).

"To me," Susan wrote about her late father in *Easy Street,* "this is a story of a father who was a gangster, not a gangster who was a father."

Even knowing what she knew as an adult, Susan still saw her father through the eyes of a little girl. She adored him as a child, overlooking his faults, and continued to do so as an adult. Susan's father had dark hair, was 5 feet, 10 inches tall, weighed 165 pounds, but to Susan, he was larger than life, a giant of a man in her eyes. Now he was gone. For the rest of her life, Susan would be told how much she resembled her father.

Susan's mother, Gladys, was gravely ill during the last year of her life. She ultimately had a mental breakdown and was institutionalized. It was during this time that she sent her daughter to Chadwick School in Palos Verdes Peninsula in southern California. Judy Garland's daughter, Liza Minnelli, was one year behind Susan.

"Everybody at Chadwick was the son or daughter of somebody famous," Susan wrote in *Easy Street*. Dean Martin's daughters Claudia and Gail lived in Susan's dorm. Yul Brynner's son Rock was in Susan's French class. Jann Wenner, who would go on to found *Rolling Stone* magazine, was editor of the school newspaper and president of the eighth grade.

Susan *hated* Chadwick. "Never had so many young egos joined under one roof," she later wrote. The only friend she made was Susan Amateau, daughter of Hollywood television writer and director Rod Amateau. "I stayed in my dorm room most days to avoid the sun and wrote," Susan said in *Easy Street*. That is, until she befriended Susan. "I thought Susan [Amateau] was the most intelligent person I had ever met," Susan wrote. "She read Shakespeare, used big words, and wrote poetry. She was the leader of the Bohemian crowd and I was terribly honored to be her friend. She called me

Bermouse, because I was so silent, and included me in early morning poetry readings on the lawn."

Susan's celebrity prep school included on its roster alums Robert Towne, Brandon Lee, and Mike Lookinland (of TV's "Brady Bunch"). Immortalized in the book and made-for-TV movie *Mommie Dearest,* Chadwick was where Joan Crawford's daughter Christina was sent, with unhappy results.

After Gladys committed suicide while living in a rest home, Susan's Uncle Chickie sent her to St. Helen's Hall, an expensive boarding school, albeit an Episcopal one, in Portland, Oregon. With Davie gone, Chickie could no longer afford the opulent life that had been provided for Davie's only daughter. Still, Chickie scraped together the tuition, mostly through gambling winnings or loans, and tried to raise Susan in the manner in which she had been accustomed.

It was at St. Helen's Hall that Susan began to learn of her father's mob activities. She read, over a boy's shoulder, a *Los Angeles Times* article about Gus Greenbaum's gangland-style murder. The paper was reporting that, on December 3, 1958, police discovered Greenbaum dead in bed, his throat cut so completely that his head nearly fell off.

Down the hall, in a different bedroom, officers found Greenbaum's dead wife, her throat cut as well. The wife had been knocked out with a heavy bottle which caved in the right side of her eye. Newspapers were piled around her to keep the blood from staining the carpet.

Susan's classmate told her, "The gangsters, they run Las Vegas and kill each other and the way you know if you're going to die is they put a picture of a black hand on your bed."

The thought terrified Susan.

For the rest of Susan's life, the desert—the good *and* the bad—would haunt her. She would always feel robbed of the good life she'd felt was her birthright and one she'd been spoiled with as a child. She never got over losing her parents and being yanked out of the Las Vegas childhood she had so enjoyed. It would carry over into her later work as a journalist, author, and screenwriter. For the rest of her life, she would miss her father. She sought solace in a surrogate figure, a young man named Bobby Durst, whom she would meet during her college years who would become a big brother to her—a best friend—and play a large role in her life.

Susan was haunted not only by her childhood and the void of not having parents, but by Las Vegas itself.

"The man I grew up with in Las Vegas adored the town, loved the town," Susan said during her A&E network interview. "I often looked at Las Vegas as an older sibling I had to compete with. All I know is, every morning he woke up and said, 'It's 80 degrees outside. How bad can it be?'"

In *Lady Las Vegas*, Susan wrote: "In the beginning, I adored her, that Lady Las Vegas, my fantastic, world-famous, older sister—who could ever compare? Even though my father, the famed Las Vegas hotel-casino pioneer Davie Berman, had her just one year before my birth, she had 40 years of sophistication, glamour and class on me. As I grew up, I began to envy her. Did my dad like her better, prefer her? She intrigued him, magnetized his interest, and earned his constant praise."

One summer, while still in high school, Susan's Uncle Chickie sent her to the prestigious Monticeto-Sequoia Camp for Girls. Also attending was Julie Nixon. Susan and Julie played leads together in *Little Women*. Nothing was too good for Davie Berman's precious daughter. Susan treated herself the same way. She would always manage to live in an exclusive neighborhood.

Later, she moved just off the famed Sunset Strip for five years, in a friend's apartment, rent free. And, ultimately, she lived in Benedict Canyon in a house where she couldn't afford to keep up with the rent. Susan spent two lengthy stays in the leased house, which, ironically, was just two miles from where Susan's father's partner, Ben "Bugsy" Siegel, was murdered in 1947 in the Moorish-style Beverly Hills house rented by Virginia Hill, at 810 Linden Drive. Some have said Siegel's associates, including Davie Berman, ordered the hit. After Siegel's murder, newspaper reporters following the case wrote that Siegel "had an arrest record like a village phone book." It was front-page news across America. Nine bullets were fired from a 30-caliber army carbine, police determined at the time.

Vegas was a small town when Bugsy Siegel and

Davie Berman first rolled into the desert in the 1940s and started the Flamingo, with Meyer Lansky and Lucky Luciano's money. Gangsters built Vegas in the real world and ran it until the FBI ran them out in the 1970s and '80s. It was a world Susie knew from the inside. Susan Berman was a Mafia princess in her childhood, with the Flamingo Hotel as her playground.

Bugsy once described the Flamingo to a reporter as "the goddamn biggest, fanciest gaming casino and hotel you bastards ever seen in your whole lives."

The Bermans lived a first-class existence. Theirs was the lifestyle of old, moneyed Las Vegas, the type of life portrayed in Universal Pictures' hit movie *Casino*, based on the life of a mobster. Davie Berman coddled and protected his daughter. It was not until later that Susan learned the truth about what really went on behind her family's life in the desert. She later would turn her childhood tales of hobnobbing with Mafia players and high-rolling gamblers into a series of successful books and documentaries.

Davie Berman couldn't do enough for his daughter. For her eighth birthday, he gave her a vintage slot machine. As her school schedule allowed, he took her to work with him. It was almost as if he'd known that his days were numbered. He wanted to spend as much time with her as he could—and he did. Susie was constantly by his side, both in and out of the casinos.

In those days, Davie was called the "ambassador of gambling." He worked in the pit overseeing the tables where seated were entertainers Jack Benny and Jimmy Durante, producer Harry Cohn, prominent businessmen, foreign dignitaries, and Las Vegas's highest rollers. Susan walked beside her father, a man who was forceful and feared, unknowingly living in a world that was dangerous and violent. The family didn't have a bank account; they paid cash for everything, and the money seemed endless. Davie Berman neither gambled nor drank. He invariably wore expensive suits and French cologne. Hanging from his pocket was a ruby mezuzah on a gold chain. Davie greeted customers by their first names, making them feel welcome and at home in his joints. He was a respectable gangster casino operator. He drove a fancy new Cadillac. To his Susie, he was the world.

What Susan didn't know then was that when mob families were feuding, her family was in danger. During mob unrest, Davie piloted Susan away to Los Angeles and the Beverly Wilshire Hotel for two or three days, telling her it was for a short vacation. Bodyguard Lou Raskin lived with the Bermans so he could watch over Davie's precious daughter. Susie thought the trips were family vacations and loved the ice-cream sundaes from room service.

Susan's mother often told her, "If anyone asks if you're Davie Berman's daughter, say, 'No.' Run, scream for Lou, yell, use whatever you have to do to get away. You go nowhere with no one." Susan told

A&E network, "It was almost an obnoxious drill to a kid, I heard it so many times."

Lou was a large man her father hired to watch over his daughter. "Lou was always seated in the front room," Susan said. "I don't know if my father would have considered him a bodyguard, but he was basically my gin partner. I was playing gin and beating him from the time I was three, and I thought that was his sole purpose."

Gladys Berman's worst nightmare, that her daughter would be kidnapped, became a reality in 1955 when Susan was 10. She was in front of the Fifth Street School, where she was enrolled, when a middle-aged man dragged a kicking and screaming Susan into a waiting car. He tossed Susan onto the backseat of the sedan with a bunch of comic books.

Susan wrote the following in *Easy Street* about her abduction: "He [the man] had only driven a block when I hit him in the face and jumped out of the car yelling all the way. Two policemen heard me and brought me home. It was a blow my mother's friends say she never recovered from. There was no evidence it was a Mob kidnap; it could have been a crank or a pervert. But it happened to be a time of Mob tension. My mother was convinced that I had just escaped death."

The kidnapper no doubt would have faced a death sentence, had he been caught by Susan's father. Davie was once described on the front page of the *New York Times* by an NYPD detective as "the toughest Jew I ever met." A reporter once said Davie

Berman was "so tough he could kill a man with one hand tied behind his back." And an FBI file said that Berman was "a trained killer." Davie Berman had a notorious reputation in law enforcement circles because of his involvement in a kidnap-for-ransom and bank robbery spree in New York during Prohibition in the 1920s.

It was a more than colorful life for a child. But Susan's parents went to great extremes to shelter their daughter from the seedy side of that life. The notorious Davie Berman was not the man Susan knew as a father. Davie was devoted to his family, and he made certain that his daughter was kept unaware of his unlawful enterprises. They sheltered her and spoiled her at the same time.

Susan's childhood was spent around famous entertainers. Her father arranged for Elvis Presley and Liberace to sing at her birthday parties. A month before Davie Berman died, he threw his daughter a lavish 12th-birthday party at the Riviera. Liberace sang "Happy Birthday" to her. In order to produce friends for the party, Davie invited the daughters of other Las Vegas hotel operators and owners, kids Susan barely knew. Her father wanted to fill up her party with girls her age, to make her happy.

And there were other performers in her life. "There were a few entertainers my father absolutely adored," Susan told A&E, "Danny Thomas, Jack Benny, Jimmy Durante. They were always over at our house, or we were talking to them [at the hotel].

In fact, my father had a silver dollar made. One side was a silver dollar and the other side said his name in Hebraic script, and he gave one to Jack Benny. He wore one, and he gave one to Durante. He wasn't Jewish, but he wore it as a sign of interfaith or something."

Other top stars who played the Flamingo and Riviera were the Ritz Brothers, the Andrew Sisters, Tony Martin, Frankie Lane, Kay Starr, Sophie Tucker, Spike Jones, Ken Murray and the Blackouts, Dean Martin and Jerry Lewis, Peggy Lee, Xavier Cugat, Ben Blue, the Mills Brothers, and the Ink Spots. And Susie Berman knew them all.

Susan preferred afternoons spent in the showroom watching the chorus line rehearse at her father's Flamingo Hotel over playing with her classmates from the Fifth Street School a block away from her house. She often played dress up backstage with the showgirls' costumes or swam in the Flamingo's pool. And she'd sing "Sunny Side of the Street." When she told her father she wanted to be a chorus girl when she grew up, he told her, "You're too smart to be one. You're going to college."

"As soon as school was out," Susan wrote in *Easy Street*, "summer became The Pool.... My entire summer wardrobe was two bathing suits ('Hang the wet one in the bathroom, Susie') and a flowered swimming cap....

"Our mothers drank ice tea with a slice of orange and lemon on a toothpick in it. We swam laps, did back dives, upset hotel guests, whom we laughed at because they burned so badly, and frolicked in the water."

While not golfing in his spare time, a new floor show opened at the Flamingo every two weeks and Susie's father took her to it.

"My favorite second act was the Apache dance team," Susan wrote in *Easy Street*. "My father's favorite chorus line was 'Sioux City Sue.' He never missed a performance of a new rendition of that song and I used to wonder then why he liked it so well."

Susan lived in Las Vegas when the first atomic bomb was detonated for testing in January 1951, 70 miles northeast of town. Susie was just five, but she remembered it well. The blasts were offered up by the casinos and feds as an evening of entertainment.

"The *Las Vegas Sun* ran articles, and also the *Review-Journal*, on how to treat your collectibles during the blast," Susan told A&E. "It was never thought it could hurt people." According to their accounts, "Atomic dust fallout posed the biggest danger to your vases," she said.

Susan's father stressed education for his only child. She had vivid memories of her father teaching her math in the casino's famous counting room, using dice first, when she was three, then as she got older, coins and cards.

As a counting lesson, Davie divided the money this way: so much for her father, so much for the government, and so much for mob boss Meyer Lansky. Susan unwittingly learned the ways—and the skimming habits her father practiced—of the underworld players. Skimming was a way for casino operators to pocket tax-free profits from the daily takes.

"The skimming, of course," Susan told A&E, "it was a crime, but it wasn't a crime like having to kill people. In their minds, they cheated the government.

"I was in the famous counting room, and I saw them go, 'Three for us, one for the government, and two for Meyer.' I helped them count the bills. My father taught me to count basically on dice, when I was very little, two or three, and on cards."

Not for one moment did Susie suspect that this doting father, thoughtful employer and star citizen could possibly have been instrumental in running the Murder, Inc. in Las Vegas for out-of-town mob bosses. Nor did any other family members question his activities. The generous Davie regularly distributed money to his unsuspecting relatives, paying particular attention to his aging parents and his sister, Lillian Berman Minter. When Lillian married, Davie footed the bill for an extravagant wedding.

It would not be until Susan attended college that the truth would begin sinking in about her father and his lifetime association with the underworld.

Susan Berman's high-class world was shattered—and the glitz and glamour along with it— when her dad's heart failed two days before Father's Day, June 18, 1957. Davie Berman died in a hospital during a surgical procedure to remove a rectal polyp. Davie always told Susie, "Nothing can hurt you. You're my girl." Now he was gone. Who would protect her? Her ailing mother, who for years had been in and out of a mental hospital? Not likely. Susan was devastated. And she felt alone.

A cloud had washed over Susan's happy childhood. The rich Vegas lifestyle—and her security—slipped away with her father. Life as she knew it would never be the same.

When her father died Susan's uncle held her and said, "Susie, cry now, not later. You're going to have to be tough to survive." She later wrote, "I cried for the life I would know no more, cried for my father who would not live to see his only child grow up, and cried most of all because I forgot to tell him I loved him and now it was much too late."

Davie Berman's funeral at the time was the largest ever in Las Vegas history. Thousands of mourners attended. Davie Berman, dead at 54, lay in an open casket. Susan, just 12 years old, stood stoic next to her father's casket, alongside mourners in the crime syndicate's upper crust. Then, she tried to jump into the casket and drape her body over her father's lifeless one. The pallbearers stopped her.

In *Lady Las Vegas*, Susan wrote that she despised Las Vegas. "By the age of 12," she wrote, "I hated her [Las Vegas] with every fiber of my being and I held her responsible for the terrible tragedy that befell my family and orphaned me."

Davie's partners and associates served as his pallbearers, people like racketeer Gus Greenbaum (who was later decapitated), convicted extortionist

Willie "the Ice Pick" Alderman, who would die serving time in Terminal Island on a mob extortion rap, noted gambler Nick "The Greek" Dandolos, a famed odds maker, and Davie Berman's business partner Joe "Bowser" Rosenberg, who was known as Davie's mouthpiece.

Susan wrote about what happened afterward. "After my father's death," she wrote, "the whole town [Las Vegas] went crazy. First they thought he had been murdered. One man told me, 'There was an emergency meeting of all of us. When we heard Davie went down, we were furious. If some bastard had killed him we planned to murder him and his family for this. Nobody could kill Davie Berman and get away with it. He belonged to us. He was our mainstay here, he was number one. It was a bad time for us, real bad, I remember that day, men I had never seen shed a tear crying. In our business we don't really love each other, but we all loved Davie.'"

During the funeral, the rabbi told mourners: "It is a sad day for all of Las Vegas. Davie Berman, one of our original pioneers who made this city bloom, is dead. There will never be anyone like him. Davie Berman had a vision. He saw a boomtown where others had just seen desert. He was Mr. Las Vegas. Davie Berman, beloved by all of Las Vegas, beloved husband and beloved father, is gone."

Years later her father's friends told her, "Davie, boy, was he crazy about you!"

Mourners grabbed Susie, kissed her, and told her, "Susie, your dad was the greatest gangster that ever lived. You can hold your head up high." It was the first time Susie heard her father referred to as a gangster. Another mourner told her, "Your dad was a stand up guy." She didn't know then that stand up guy meant someone who would not crack under pressure.

The men's words would haunt Susan for the rest of her days. She would spend her life writing about Las Vegas and researching her father's ties to the Mafia.

Within hours of Davie Berman's funeral, the same men who acted as pallbearers at his funeral cleaned out the Berman house and gave away most of Susan's toys. When she was shipped off to Idaho to live with her Uncle Chickie, she took with her just a single trunk load of clothes, mementos, and sou-venirs—the things her father's partners had packed up. Susan never learned what happened to the rest of her family's belongings.

The day after Davie's death, an obituary ran in the June 19th edition of the *Los Angeles Times*, headlined "Las Vegas Hotel Man Dave Berman, 53, Dies." The obit read:

> David (Dave) Berman, 53, Las Vegas hotel-man and one of the principal owners of the Riviera Hotel there, died yesterday morning after surgery in Rose de Lima Hospital, Henderson, Nev. Mr. Berman had been ill only a week.
>
> Funeral services will be conducted in Las Vegas at 11 a.m. today and a memorial service will be con-ducted in Los Angeles at 2 p.m. tomorrow in the Home of Peace Mausoleum Chapel.

Mr. Berman was active in the Nevada hotel business for many years and was one of the group which owned and operated the Flamingo Hotel in Las Vegas prior to his connection with the Riviera.

He leaves a widow, Gladys, and daughter, Susan, 12, of Las Vegas.

And on the same day, the *Las Vegas Sun* ran this front-page obituary:

Funeral Rites Here Today For Dave Berman, 53

Funeral services will be conducted at Bunker Bros. Mortuary at 11 a.m. today for Dave Berman, 53, one of the pioneers in the Las Vegas casino business, who died of a heart attack yesterday at Rose de Lima Hospital where he was recovering from a glandular operation.

Berman was one of the active owners and operators at the Riviera Hotel where he was associated with Gus Greenbaum, Benny Goffstein, Joe Rosenberg, and Willie Alderman. Moving from the Flamingo to the Riviera, Berman and his associates took over the floundering hotel and made an outstanding success of the venture.

Following the local services to be conducted by Rabbi Arthur B. Leibowitz, Berman's body will be sent to Los Angeles where services will be held at 2 p.m. tomorrow at the Home of the Peace in Boyle Heights. He is survived by his wife, Gladys, his 12-year-old daughter Susan, his brother Charles Berman of Lewiston, Idaho, and sister Mrs. Maurice Minter, of Minneapolis, Minn.

Berman entered the Henderson hospital last Wednesday for major surgery and was making a satisfactory recovery at the time of the heart attack. Doctors said that there was no connection between the heart condition and the surgery. He succumbed about 7 a.m. yesterday.

Berman was well known for his philanthropies—many of them performed anonymously—which came to light later only by accident. One of them, for example, was the little known occasion when Berman won a luxurious Cadillac after buying many $100 tickets on a Variety Club drawing. He refused to accept the car, telling the officers to sell the Cadillac and put the money in the club to help handicapped children. He was always willing to help out charitable organizations. In addition to being a member of the Variety Club he was a major fund raiser for the City of Hope Hospital.

Berman had an outstanding war record. In 1942 he entered the Canadian Army; serving overseas, he fought with distinction at Anzio, Sicily, and throughout the entire Italian campaign. He was honorably discharged in 1945.

Immediately thereafter, Berman came to Las Vegas. He was part owner and associate in four clubs besides the Riviera. In 1945 he was connected with the El Cortez Hotel. In 1946 with the Las Vegas Club and El Dorado (now the Horseshoe); and in 1947 he became interested in the Flamingo Hotel.

Berman watched Las Vegas grow from a fledgling gambling town to one of the world's most glamorous resort centers. It was partly through his vision and industriousness that it became what it is today, according to his close associates.

Berman was born Jan. 16, 1903, in Ashley, North Dakota.

(Both obits incorrectly reported Davie's age as 53. He was 54.)

In 1959, a year and a half after her father's funeral, Susan was told her mother had died of a heart attack. Later, however, Susan learned that her mother in actuality had committed suicide from an overdose of drugs. Her death certificate said "suicide by overdose." Gladys was overcome with grief at the loss of her husband.

Susan, at just 13 years old, was an orphan.

She was suddenly whisked away from Las Vegas and the life she'd spent unknowingly surrounded by the mob. Susan held onto her visions of the desert she grew up in. Her images of her mother were vivid. She remembered that each New Year's Eve, her glamorous mother, a former tap dancer famous for her "Pennies From Heaven" routine, would sparkle as she performed on a Las Vegas stage in one of Davie's casinos. The memories of Susan's father were that of a quiet, hardworking casino operator who doted on and loved his only daughter with all his heart.

The orphaned 13-year-old Susan was shuffled off to Idaho to live with her uncle Chickie, her father's younger brother, then to a boarding school in Portland, Oregon. Chickie was a once-notable gambler and bookie. Although her uncle was good to her and Susan adored him, she missed her parents terribly.

Chickie became a broken man, never fully recovering from the loss of his big brother. He had always been a compulsive gambler. With Davie gone, there was no one to get him out of scrapes, like the time

Davie bailed out Chickie, after gambling away hundreds of thousands of dollars, from Benny Binion's high-stakes poker game at Benny's Vegas horse ranch on Bonanza Road, west of downtown. Benny, who founded Binion's Horseshoe Club, was known for breaking legs and shooting men if they didn't make good on their gambling debts. Davie was always there for his baby brother, regardless of the trouble.

Binion's oldest son Jack later told Susan Berman, "I remember we saw your dad the day before he went in for that operation that killed him. He was always so nice to me. I was just a kid. My dad says to him, 'If you're having stomach problems it's because your money belt is ingrown.' Your dad laughed. When we found out he had died, we just couldn't believe it."

Chickie ended up living in cheap Las Vegas motel rooms, then in and out of hospitals, where he died. But he kept enough money aside for Susan to continue attending an expensive boarding school alongside children of means and wealth, then later sent her to college. That was what Davie would have wanted.

Chapter 3

Davie Berman and the Jewish Mob

He passed on to me his greatest quality: strength.
Strength, because maybe he knew that one day I
would find out who he had really been and then I
would need every bit of strength I had to survive.
—Susan Berman
from *Easy Street*

WITH BUGSY SIEGEL'S arrival in Las Vegas in 1945, Jewish gangsters began running the desert town.

Back in the 1940s and 1950s, "The Jewish Mob *was* Las Vegas," said Myram Borders, who grew up a decade before Susan Berman in the same neighborhood, and who, like Susan, became a journalist. "The Jewish mob ran this town. No one had even heard of the Italian mob."

"It was the Jews, by and large," wrote author Norman Cantor in *The Jewish Experience*, "not the Italians, who created what was later called the Mafia. In the 1920s the Italians began to replace the Jews in the New York organized crime industry, but as late as 1940 if you wanted a spectacular hit you were looking for a representative of the Lepke Buchalter Gang, also known as Murder Inc. Jews were also prominent in the gambling trade and developed Las Vegas in the 1940s. It was a Jewish gambler who fixed the 1919 baseball World Series—which became known as the Black Sox scandal."

In Wallace Turner's book *Gambler's Money*, he quoted what he described as an "anonymous high government official" as saying, "Some of the places in Las Vegas today are really controlled by the Mafia and we know this because we see some of their muscle men around. But the front men are almost always Jews."

Robert Lacey, in *Little Man: Meyer Lansky and the Gangster Life*, wrote, "Las Vegas offered Meyer Lansky the second great chance in his life to go legit, but he made no special effort to take it. Several dozen former bootleggers, bookies, and carpet-joint operators flooded into Las Vegas from different corners of America in the late 1940s, seizing the opportunity to sidestep their pasts—and most of Ben Siegel's co-investors in the El Cortez fell into this category. Gus Greenbaum was an Arizona bookmaker. Willie Alderman and the Berman brothers, Davie and Chickie, had run carpet joints in Minneapolis."

Despite his notorious background, Davie kept a low profile in Las Vegas. Unlike their Italian counterparts, no Jewish mobster wanted his children to follow in his footsteps and go into his "business." In contrast to "retired" Italian Mafia leaders, Jewish mobsters were loath to grant interviews to the media. They didn't like to see their names in print.

In part, it had to do with the awareness that their activities could bring shame to their families and the Jewish community. It explained why Davie Berman, an important part of Vegas history, intentionally stayed out of the limelight.

Most Jewish gangsters did all they could to keep their offspring and families totally separated and uninvolved in their illegal enterprises. For instance, Meyer Lansky kept his family ignorant of what he did for a living and was proud of the fact that his younger son, Paul, graduated from New York City's elite Horace Mann School and from West Point. Longy Zwillman was painfully aware that his family and children suffered because of what he was. He dissociated his relatives from his activities, finding them jobs in legitimate businesses. The bootlegger Waxey Gordon made certain his family remained ignorant of his unlawful enterprises and sent his children to the best private schools and universities. And the FBI acknowledged that the notorious Louis "Lepke" Buchalter was devoted to his family, kept them unaware of his activities, and provided for his stepson's college education. West Coast hoodlum Mickey Cohen spoke for that generation of Jewish mobsters when he maintained: "We had a code of ethics like the ones among bankers, other people in other walks of life, that one never involved his wife or family in his work."

The Last Frontier casino opened in 1942. Next came the Flamingo, and with it Bugsy Siegel and organized crime to Las Vegas. During the 1950s, hotel building took off at a feverish pace. Each hotel owner tried to outdo its predecessors in opulence. The unbridled growth of what would later be called the Strip divided Las Vegas casinos into two basic categories: "carpet joints" and "sawdust joints." Sawdust on the floors was replaced with carpet.

The Flamingo had redefined gambling joints. It was a high-class carpet joint. Gone were tobacco-chewing men in cowboy hats and boots. People, instead, dressed up to gamble. Las Vegas was becoming sophisticated. Davie Berman helped run the higher-end carpet joints.

Despite their gangster backgrounds, Davie and the Jewish mob brought glamour and class to the casinos.

The Mafia needed Vegas for two reasons: to take control of legal gambling, and to launder money from their varied and nefarious enterprises. In the early days, there was no Strip, just downtown's seedy Glitter Gulch and a few small casinos sprinkled along the two-lane Los Angeles Highway. The town was small, and when the wind kicked up, it was a dust bowl. The streets of downtown were still dirt, except for parts of Seventh Street and Fifth Street. Sixth and Seventh streets were where mob-connected families like the Bermans chose to live. It was considered a nicer section of town.

With the nod from their East Coast bosses and the promise to give them 25 percent of everything they took in, the partners bought their first downtown club, named the El Cortez. Davie Berman brought in his best friend, Willie Alderman, and joined another old friend, Moe Sedway, in the partnership. Bugsy, in turn, brought in Gus Greenbaum, a leading bookie from Phoenix. The partners bought and ran two other downtown casinos: the Las Vegas Club and the El Dorado. As the pit boss, Davie owned 11 percent of the combined take. Bugsy owned 25 percent. Gus and Willie each had 10 percent. The rest belonged to the bosses. Each day, Davie watched over the shares, set credit limits for gamblers, and supervised the games.

As soon as word spread that Vegas was a success, gangsters from Chicago, Detroit, Cleveland, and Los Angeles began to muscle their way in. There was an influx of mobsters from Los Angeles because of the constant police crackdowns there. Davie became known as a mob diplomat, setting up liaisons between aspiring opportunists and East Coast bosses. But he had to fight constantly to protect his and his partners' hometown turf. Las Vegas was their town and they made sure that outsiders understood that and kept their distance.

Early on, Bugsy Siegel had convinced Meyer Lansky that he could expand south, away from downtown, by putting a hotel out on the two-lane U.S. Highway 91, later called Los Angeles Highway, and transform it into a gambling palace. It was a strong draw for tourists worldwide, including Hollywood celebrities. Lansky bought out all but a few shares of William Wilkerson's interest in a new half-built hotel. It was called the Flamingo and was surrounded by desert on the south end of the highway. Bugsy got the nod from his bosses, finished construction, and opened the Flamingo in 1946. But the hotel was still unfinished and in debt.

On top of that, Hollywood stars couldn't attend the grand opening because of a rainstorm in Los Angeles. The so-called opening was a public relations disaster. As a result, Bugsy never showed a profit. Before Bugsy could prove himself and turn a profit, he was shot and killed gangland style in June of 1947. His murder was never solved. It was widely believed that the syndicate bosses had ordered Bugsy to liquidate and when he refused, they ordered his death. A lot of people in Las Vegas, including Davie Berman, were at one time rumored to have actually pulled the trigger on the gun used to kill Bugsy. That was impossible, though, because within five minutes of his death, while Los Angeles police were still arriving at the house in Beverly Hills, and long before any official news of Ben's murder reached Las Vegas, four men marched into the lobby of the Flamingo—Dave Berman, Gus Greenbaum, Willie Alderman, and Moe Sedway— and took control of the casino. There were fierce sandstorms tearing through the sky that night, and the casino was half empty. It stopped operating for five minutes of silence in Bugsy's honor. Then control of the Las Vegas syndicate fell on Davie and his partners. Within six months, the Flamingo was showing a profit. The partners used whatever force necessary to retain their hold on their empire.

On the outside, Davie appeared to be a generous philanthropist and a model citizen, promoting Las Vegas and engaging in civic and Jewish activities. He moved in the same circles as top entertainers and powerful people, such as the mayor and the town's sheriff. Davie had become an integral member of the Jewish mob, Meyer Lansky's first lieutenant, and confidant to Frank Costello, but also a well-respected casino mogul.

Susan Berman's life in the underworld began in Las Vegas in 1945, still an isolated, dusty desert town. After they arrived, Davie, Gladys, and Susie stayed in El Rancho Vegas's yellow and blue low-hotel, which was more like an expanded motor inn. With its then-towering windmill on the Strip, it attracted hordes of guests and celebrities. The Bermans stayed there for several months until Susan's mother found a house at 721 South Sixth Street, which they bought. Most mob and casino operatives lived on South Sixth or nearby, buying up small houses spread over a couple of blocks. Susan regularly climbed a big tree in the front yard and played in a large playhouse—practically the size of a small bungalow—at the back of their property, behind their house. Her father was set financially and gave his only child whatever she wanted.

Vegas has no memory—only the present—and Davie Berman, a convicted and notorious kidnapper-robber-gangster from the Syndicate in Minneapolis, took advantage of his new town's unusual trait. He gained respectability.

One way the mobsters back then did this was to put their names in the phone directory, just like every other citizen in town. Davie was listed under "Berman, Dave," with his street address and telephone number Dudley 4-1941 next to it. Even Willie Alderman was in there, at 1400 South Sixth Street, a block up the street from the Bermans. Joe Rosenberg lived at 1800 South Fourth Place (the house has since been torn down).

According to the FBI's records, file number 52755, Davie once used aliases of "Dave Berman, Charles Gordon, Charles Gorden, and Dave the Jew." In Las Vegas, he was always called Davie, although he referred to himself as "Dave." Even though he was a notorious gangster, Davie was polite.

A reporter for the *New York Times*, after a 1925 bank robbery and kidnapping involving Berman, wrote about him, saying: "The bandit was termed a gentleman *yegg* by his courtesy for his captive." The FBI tagged Davie's file, along with Gus Greenbaum's and Ben Siegel's, the "Nevada Project."

One entry in Davie's FBI file read, "The notorious Dave Berman has a reputation as a stick up man and killer. Both Dave and Chickie Berman, his brother, associate with Philip alias Flippy Scher, notorious Minneapolis killer who was recently discharged from the army and presently operates a gambling joint at 319 Nicollet, Minneapolis."

Another FBI entry said: "Davie Berman was arrested 5 May 1927 for the kidnapping of bootlegger Abe Scharlin. He received on 24 November 1927 a 12 year sentence. He would do 7.4 years in Sing Sing. He got free 15 August 1934. Berman then became the gambling czar of Minneapolis replacing Isadore Kid Cann."

Kid Cann was identified by the FBI in 1942 as "the overlord of the Minneapolis, Minnesota, underworld."

Author Robert Rockaway, in *But He Was Good to His Mother: The Lives and Crimes of Jewish Gangsters*, wrote, "Originally from Sioux Falls, Iowa, prominent Jewish gangsters in Minneapolis included 'Kid' Cann (Isador Blumenfeld), Yiddie Bloom, and the Berman brothers, Davie and Chickie. Cann is believed to have been responsible for the murder of Walter Ligget, publisher of *Midwest America*, for a series of articles the paper printed about the Minneapolis criminal underworld. Ligget was gunned down in front of his family while Christmas shopping. Much of illicit [Minneapolis] business was managed by Isadore 'Kid' Cann... Blumenfeld and his all-Jewish syndicate."

It took Susan nearly a year to get her father's FBI files through the Freedom of Information Act. Prior to receiving the files, a clerk at FBI headquarters in Washington, D.C., was assigned to read through them before releasing copies to Susan. She asked the clerk about her father.

"At one point," Susan wrote, "I asked timidly, 'Do

you have any information that he killed anyone?' 'Oh, yes,' the clerk answered in her cheerful impersonal way, 'He was a trained killer.'"

Las Vegas was a chance for a new start for Davie. Susan commented in her A&E documentary, "My father and all his friends were criminals from the time they were 11 or 12 years old. He had served eight years of hard time in Sing Sing. So I think for many of these men, Las Vegas was their last chance, Las Vegas was their *only* chance, and they were determined, in their 40s, to do it right. They didn't want any trouble with the government and they didn't want any crime in Las Vegas."

After Pearl Harbor, Davie Berman tried to join the service, to fight for his country. But he was an ex-felon and was denied. So he and Charles Barron, a bootlegger and gambler from Chicago, drove to Winnipeg and enlisted in the Canadian Army, the 18th Armored Car Regiment of the 12th Manitoba Dragons, a reconnaissance unit nicknamed "Princess Pat." Davie earned the rank of lance corporal. He ended up going to Britain with the 1st Canadian Division Support Battalion as a machine gun loader and wireless operator. Susan's mother Gladys, during her husband's absence, joined the Women's Army Corps along with 150,000 American women who served during World War II. After being injured in Anzio, Sicily, behind German lines, Davie Berman was honorably discharged on August 16, 1944. The Canadian government awarded him the Italy Star, the Defense Medal, the Canadian

Volunteer Service Medal, and a plot of ground in Canada, which Davie donated to a Jewish organization.

Davie returned to Minneapolis, to his wife, and to the rackets. The next year, Susan was born and the family relocated to the Nevada desert, where her father invested in casinos, starting on May 10, 1945.

Gangsters' pasts could be shed like a lizard skin in the desert. Comedian Alan King, who worked in Las Vegas in the 1950s, told A&E, "No one talked about the background of the owners or the casino managers, or whatever. Vegas was like another planet. All of a sudden, the things that were illegal all over the country became not only acceptable, it was what drove the town."

It was the start of Las Vegas's glory days. Mobsters, billionaires, politicians, gamblers, and movie stars all sought solace in the desert. The Flamingo represented the new and enticing Las Vegas.

"Las Vegas could not have been Las Vegas," Dennis McBride, a historian and author who grew up in the desert town, told A&E, "if it had not been for the mob."

Rod Amateau, now retired from TV writing and directing, agreed, telling A&E that the mob moved alongside entertainers. "Those were the days of the Reds," he said, "Red Skelton, Redd Foxx, and Red Buttons, and large, heavy Jewish men with little-boy names—Henny, Snooky, Youngie, Beepy, Booky,

Boppy. You know, little names. Little names for big guys."

After meeting Ben Siegel for the first time, someone walked up afterward to Amateau and told him, "You know, he's a gangster." Amateau replied, "Well, you know, as long as he doesn't shoot me, I'm not gonna judge him; everybody's gotta make a living."

Violent crimes in the gangsters new town were committed outside the state line. "There was to be no killing in Las Vegas," Susan said in her A&E documentary. "The story is always told, and I'm sure it's true, about two men who robbed the casino. All the owners followed them to the state line and killed them because there is no crime in Vegas."

Las Vegas was an unofficial no-kill zone. Mobsters could continue their skimming while local lawmen turned their heads, just as long as they didn't commit murder inside the Nevada state line. With the Nevada-California state line just 40 miles south of Las Vegas, the order was easy for mobsters to follow.

Bob Stupak, a casino operator who developed the Stratosphere Tower, chuckled when he told A&E, "Back then, it was like we had two police forces. We had regular police and then we had the boys. [It was] one of the few cities in the country that had two police forces, you know, and that took care of everything."

Debbie Reynolds, a mainstay Las Vegas entertainer from the Rat Pack days, explained it most succinctly when she told A&E: "I don't say I respect how they got their money. It's none of my business anyway. That was for Elliot Ness to handle. [But] no one got killed who wasn't supposed to be. And we never were frightened or anything of that sort." She commented that she missed "that loyalty, that respect," because of the courteous way "the boys" treated female entertainers in the early days.

Because Nevada legalized gambling in 1931, for people like Davie Berman and Benjamin Siegel, it was a desert oasis with a promising and lucrative future. Davie was convinced that it was the only place to be. He could pursue the American dream, get a second chance for his family, become respectable. And he did.

Susan's father was a good friend and business partner of Siegel's, the notorious gangster whose mob power base spread from Los Angeles across the Mohave Desert to Vegas. Davie Berman, Siegel, and Meyer Lansky were gangsters from a mostly Jewish crime syndicate. The trio pioneered the development of Las Vegas from a sleepy desert cow town to a thriving gold mine. But they soon found themselves in an uneasy alliance when the *La Cosa Nostra* firms moved in. Davie, along with his partners, ran the joint after Siegel was shot to death.

With Siegel's death, the Flamingo partners regrouped: Gus Greenbaum bought 27 percent interest; Elia Atol, 17-1/2; Joe Rosenberg, "Little Icepick" Willie Alderman, and Davie Berman, 7 percent each; Charlie "Kewpie" Rich, 2 percent; Sidney

Wyman, 10 percent; and Jack McElroy, 4 percent. Then Gus gave Benny Goffstein 2 percent and named him vice president.

"Rosenberg was made casino manager and Dave Berman, who could kill a man with one hand, was suddenly everywhere, barking orders, scowling ferociously, and getting things done in a hurry," according to the book the *Green Felt Jungle*. During the first year the new partners managed the Flamingo, it showed a profit of $4 million dollars. Ten years later, Davie Berman was dead. Three years after that, Gus Greenbaum was murdered.

In 1971, the Flamingo Hotel was purchased by the Hilton Hotel Corporation and renamed the Flamingo Hilton. The mob no longer ran it.

Dick Odessky, a former journalist and now an author, went to work as a public relations man for the Flamingo in 1961 and remembered its heyday. Before he worked at the hotel, he was a newspaper entertainment columnist who covered hotels and casinos. He got to know the players.

"I went back to Los Angeles as a newspaper man at the L.A. *Herald Examiner*, then in '61, I went to work at the Flamingo," Odessky said in an interview from his California home. "Morris Lansburgh had just taken it over. It was still a Lansky property. Lansky kept it until Lansburgh left in '67. With the Jewish mob back then you never knew with them who was big and who wasn't. Lansky was boss. He was boss of the Mafia. Lucky Luciano was the *big* boss. When he was deported, he put Lansky in.

Davie and the boys were operators for Lansky. There were different organizations and we didn't learn of some of them until much later.

"The Jewish mob was very heavy into book making. The Italians were in with the Jews. It was a co-arrangement. They weren't fighting each other."

Odessky knew Davie Berman.

"I had met Davie Berman," he said. "I stayed away from the Flamingo earlier because Gus Greenbaum scared the heck out of me. He was as frightening looking a man as I'd ever known. One day I was told Gus wanted to see me. I tried every possible way not to have to see him. I saw him. He told me they were going to build a silo out in front that could be seen from the California border. They built it and it could be seen only from the Tropicana [Avenue on the Strip]. Davie stayed in the background. During that whole time the big guys, the hoods, were all my friends. They were all looking out for me. I wasn't even old enough at that time to *be* in the casinos. I was 19. They kind of adopted me. Ned Day [the late reporter who covered the mob] always would come to me when I was still writing at the *Valley Times*. He'd come to me and say, 'How do you get in to see these people?' I told him, 'You don't just walk in. You've got to get respect from them.' He said, 'You walk into every door in this town.' I told him, 'Notice where I *don't* walk. You never see me with the feds, do you?' I told him, 'The boys don't like that. You can't play one side against the other.'

"The feds tried to court me going all the way back

to '53. They wanted me to watch for somebody. I told them I wouldn't do it. Because of that, the boys had a lot more respect for me."

After Susan learned about her father's role in the mob, she wrote in *Easy Street*, "My loyalty to him is just as strong as his loyalty was to his way of life, whether or not my attitude is rational. He was involved in a kill-or-be-killed world. I have more questions about my own ethics in not being able to judge him in any way for those acts than I do about his committing them.... It's a dilemma I will be struggling with for a long, long time."

Chapter 4

Susan's College Years

SUSAN CHOSE TO live an honest life, far removed from the one her father led in Vegas. Susan graduated in June 1964 with honors from St. Helen's Hall High School, taking home a certificate from the National Honors Society.

For graduation, Susan's Uncle Chickie sent her a ticket to Idaho to visit him. Once there, he told her he was sending her away for the summer, to the United Synagogue Youth Pilgrimage tour. She spent the summer in Israel.

After the tour, Susan went on to college at the University of California at Los Angeles, located in Westwood, a pedestrian-friendly college town developed in the 1920s after the UCLA campus relocated there, near where Susan attended the fifth grade. With its Mediterranean-inspired architecture, Westwood is located at the entrance to the giant UCLA campus.

Susan was accepted into UCLA's Letters in Science College and was a sociology major. She had already made up her mind she was going to be a journalist, so she took writing courses.

It was a time of change for the country, what with civil rights protests of that era. UCLA was near the heart of it when the Watts Riots broke out in Los Angeles in the summer of 1965. Discrimination, equal rights, women's rights, and civil rights all became major issues.

During Susan's sophomore year, her uncle called her to tell her he was going away. He was going to prison. The *New York Times* headline at the time read, "Four Imprisoned for Stock Fraud: United Dye Case is Rested by U.S." It said that Charles Berman, 49, had pleaded innocent but had been convicted. "Four brokers and a corporation were convicted Monday of defrauding the public of $5 million through a conspiracy to sell 400,000 shares of unregistered stock of United Dye and Chemical Corporation." Federal Judge William Herlands said the conviction "brought to a close the longest trial before a jury in the history of a U.S. District Court in the country."

The article identified Chickie Berman as a broker-dealer from Lewiston, Idaho.

He was sentenced to six years in prison and a $35,000 fine. The U.S. attorney said the defendants were "classic examples of financial parasites" who had a total disregard for the small investor in their fraudulent dealings.

Fortune magazine also wrote about the scam, describing it as "The Great Sweet Grass Swindle," saying, "selling watered stock has become a difficult and intricate business. But the boiler room boys are still at it. Here's the story of a classic operation in which the victims paid $16 million for oil stocks now worth $4 million." Chickie was pinpointed as the brains behind one of the stock schemes. "Charles M. Berman," the article continued, "who for nearly 20 years had run a string of pinball machines and juke boxes in Minneapolis where he was twice arrested on charges, later dismissed for lack of evidence, of making book on the side."

Chickie was imprisoned at a maximum-security penitentiary in Lewisburg, Pennsylvania, then in La Tuna, Texas. He ultimately was transferred to Terminal Island in San Pedro, California. Susan visited him on weekends.

Back at college, Susan joined a sorority at UCLA but got kicked out after six weeks for piercing her ears. While Susan was an honors student in high school, she was an average student in college. She regularly cut classes and spent most of her spare time writing. Still, after four years, she squeaked by and obtained her undergraduate degree in education. Davie Berman would have been proud; his Susie was the first Berman to finish college.

On June 13, 1967, Susan graduated with a bachelor of arts degree. She started graduate school in September 1967 in the education department at UCLA.

In 1967 a handsome, suave—and wealthy—man walked into Susan Berman's life, where he would stay until the end. It was Bobby Durst. From the start Susan was attracted to his seemingly calm demeanor. There was something about him. They had a lot in common: both came from well-to-do fathers and had lost their mothers as children. The fact that they'd both lost their moms at young ages gave them an instant connection. Susan looked up to Bobby and talked often about him to her friends, like a proud younger sister.

Bobby Durst was also enrolled in a graduate program at UCLA, majoring in economics. Though Susan left UCLA's graduate school in March 1968, after five months and one-and-a-half quarters, Bobby stayed at UCLA until the end of June 1969. However, they remained in touch and became close friends. According to records kept by UCLA's registrar Bobby eventually walked away without getting a graduate degree.

The bond between Bobby and Susan long outlived their UCLA graduate work. They were best friends and each other's most trusted confidant. Susan was intrigued with Bobby's well-to-do background; Bobby was fascinated by Susan's mob history. While they didn't take classes together—their majors were different and they were enrolled in separate graduate programs—they'd run into each other on campus. They slowly got to know each other. They began getting together in the library and cafeteria, then off campus at local student hang-outs. He became part of Susan's inner circle of friends.

Susan transferred to the University of California at Berkeley, 350 miles north. A year earlier, Martin Luther King Jr. denounced the Vietnam War in a speech on campus at Sproul Plaza, in front of the College of Journalism building where Susan attended classes.

With student groups discussing the issues on and off both the UCLA and UCB campuses, Susan grew intellectually. She wanted to become a writer. At UC Berkeley, Susan changed her major from education to journalism and enrolled in UCB's Graduate School of Journalism, on the north end of the campus.

Berkeley during the 1960s was home of the Free Speech Movement and student radicalism. Years later, Susan would learn that the FBI had continued to track her, even after her father died, noting in its file that she was "a member of the San Francisco women's liberation and pro-abortion debater." Susan's boyfriend, Alan Neckritz, was an antiwar activist.

"She and Alan were joined at the hip," fellow student Elizabeth Mehren said. "He was a character too. He was an activist."

Back then, especially at Berkeley, anti-Vietnam protests were commonplace. Activism was rampant on campus, with anti-war and free speech rallies. According to news accounts at the time, on the afternoon of May 15, 1969, nearly 6,000 students and residents moved to reclaim People's Park, a university-owned plot of land along Telegraph Avenue that students and community members adopted as a park. Berkeley exploded. The university brought in police to repossess the park. In the ensuing riot, police and sheriff's deputies fired tear gas and buckshot at the crowd, blinding one observer and killing another. Then-Governor Ronald Reagan ordered the National Guard into Berkeley. Students continued to gather on campus and march in the days following the first riot.

"We all protested the war," said Elizabeth Mehren, who graduated with Susan. "It was a popular thing to do."

It was 1969 and the year Richard Nixon was inaugurated into office. The year before, Robert Kennedy and Martin Luther King Jr. were assassinated.

One professor, an elderly instructor, took his journalism students, including Susan, to the balcony of Sproul Hall, overlooking sit-ins, speeches, protests, and rallies. "He taught us how to count people in crowds," Mehren said. "I still use it today."

Elizabeth remembered Susan well. "She had this glamorous patina, the daughter of a mobster," she said. "Who can forget the girl who had the white Mercedes Benz at Berkeley? Here we were in Berkeley, in 1969, with National Guard troops on campus. The rest of us had crummy cars. People were driving beat-up Volkswagens. She drove a white Mercedes sedan. It was a college graduation gift [from her Uncle]. It was such a bad status symbol at Berkeley. It was almost comical. She gave you the illusion of having endless resources.

"She was an orphan. We all knew about the Riviera and the Flamingo. We all knew about Uncle Bugsy. They were part of her lore."

Among Berkeley's distinguished faculty were Nobel laureates, members of the National Academy of Sciences. Many Berkeley faculty were on the *New York Times* best-seller lists. The J-school program was an intimate one with small classes—a working collegium that put students under the direct tutorship of a group of permanent faculty, lecturers, and teaching fellows. No marketing, advertising, or public relations classes were taught there, which meant Susan was strictly learning journalism. Most of the instruction was done by journalism practitioners who continued to publish in the nation's biggest and best newspapers and magazines while teaching.

Susan honed her writing skills and was taught the craft of journalism and traditional forms of news gathering from the best in the business.

By 1969, students were demonstrating—and still being arrested by the hundreds—demanding the creation of a "Third World College."

Still, as graduation approached, Susan concentrated her time on a job search. She interviewed with a daily newspaper in San Francisco. In June 1969 she received a master's degree from UC Berkeley in the J-school's first graduating class. She had just graduated with a journalism degree from one of the best universities in the country. Her future looked bright. Fellow journalism students thought the same.

Susan befriended Edwin Bayley, the Graduate School of Journalism's first dean, beginning in 1969, and a professor emeritus there. She also got to know Bayley's wife Monica, who died in April 2002. Even then, Susan was networking, looking for ways to excel, befriending influential people who could help her. Bayley retired from UC Berkeley in 1985 and moved to Carmel, California, with his wife.

Ed Bayley saw Susan's work differently than her classmates who viewed her as a potential star. As her dean, Bayley had a different perspective, as she often went to him to discuss her journalism future, he said.

"My relationship with Susan was more of an advisor than anything else," Bayley said. "She was the kind of kid who needed a *lot* of advising. She was a big baby in a way. She put on a tough, flippant attitude and played the role of a gangster's daughter, but she was really just as soft as a baby inside. She needed a mother. She liked my wife a lot."

It was a small community of students in the J-school program, Bayley said, and everyone knew each other. "My wife and I lived in Berkeley and students came over to our house a lot," he said. "It was a smaller school. We admitted about 50 or 60 students at any one time."

"To be honest," Bayley continued, "I was critical

of her because she was always trying to find the easy way out, using gimmicks. That was the only thing I was critical of. I think she was lazy mentally that way without having to do the hard, grubby work. Then, of course, using her father's gangster status. She had a picture on her fireplace mantle of her Uncle Chickie and his girlfriend in a nightclub in Havana. Most of the time she was just a student. She had a very nice boyfriend, Alan Neckritz. He was a law student and they lived together. They were like a settled-in married couple. They used to entertain and invite faculty and other students over."

Susan lived on Hillegass Street, about eight blocks from campus. Later, she moved in, at 2555 Le Conte, with Neckritz, who today practices law in Walnut Creek, California.

Susan's personality was engaging, which made her popular on campus.

Elizabeth Mehren said Susan, however, tried to take shortcuts during college. "I hate to speak ill of the dead," Elizabeth said, "but Susan was a spoiled little girl who didn't know how to deal with life. She was marginally talented. She balked at doing a master's thesis. She didn't like the fact that she had to research topics. I was in journalism school with her and there were maybe 30 or 35 people in that class. It was very intimate. Everybody knew each other."

Mehren, too, said Susan was well liked during college.

"She had a wonderful sense of humor," Mehren said. "There was something very appealing about her. She had this vulnerability. At the same time she had this toughness.

"I'm very blond and very California. I look like a cookie-cutter California girl. So Susan and a couple of other kids in the class felt sorry for me because I didn't know anything about Jewish culture. They made me a glossary of Yiddish terms. They gave it to me for my birthday at the end of the year. However, they forgot to make it phonetic. So I mispronounced everything."

Ed Bayley said Susan struck him as being sad, even though she appeared to want for nothing. "My wife felt sorry for her," he said. "She was lonesome. She wanted to make us her mother and father. In the last letter she made a point about how much she loved us both. My wife felt sympathetic toward her more than anything else. She was not happy. She was a lonesome kid who wanted a lot of comforting. Everything she did seemed to go wrong."

After Susan was murdered, "My wife was very upset," Bayley noted. "She really liked Susie."

Lou DeCosta was in the journalism program with Susan. DeCosta, who now works in Hollywood as a story editor and writer on documentaries, also remembered Susan and her days at Berkeley.

"I was a year behind Susan," he said in a telephone interview from his L.A. home. "She was the star. She was like the golden girl. She was a great writer. She was very outgoing and self-promotional. Her reputation in school was that she was the bright star or, at least, had the potential to be the bright star if she put out the effort.... The brutal truth was that she was not an attractive woman. She was homely. But she was almost arrogant. I remember when I found out about her dad it was like a huge shock."

Susan made friends and business connections through journalism school. Later, Susan "used the J-school connection to pitch stories to Richard [Zoglin]," DeCosta said. According to DeCosta, Richard Zoglin, formerly a TV critic at *Time* magazine, now a freelance editor, dated Susan briefly. "I remember having a discussion with him. He said he hadn't seen her for a while but that she had pitched him stories."

Chapter 5
Beyond College

THE INK WAS STILL wet on her diploma when she went straight from journalism school to the staff of the then-Hearst-owned *San Francisco Examiner*.

Susan's career appeared to flourish.

Classmate DeCosta noted, "The fact that she was immediately working out of school sort of made her a hero to us."

In 1971, during her stint at the *Examiner*, Susan co-wrote and published her first book, *The Underground Guide To The College Of Your Choice*.

The *Examiner* was a good gig and a great opportunity for a cub reporter. On the surface, the future looked bright. Susan should have been on top of the world. During the course of a year, however, Susan went from being a cheerful person to a depressed one.

A key event in Susan's transformation from

cheerful to depressed occurred when she was told her mother might not have killed herself, that she could have instead been murdered by the mob—forced to take an overdose of pills—for not accepting a settlement on her father's interest in the Las Vegas hotels he had skimmed from for his East Coast bosses. Though unproven, it threw Susan into a long period of agoraphobia and manic-depression.

She lived in an apartment in Pacific Heights and had emotional difficulty just walking the six blocks to her therapist's office. She was suicidal. Something, she later wrote in *Easy Street*, forced her to stay alive. "I was all that was left of a whole family that I didn't know," she wrote. "If I died now their lives would mean nothing.... Then one day I got better, suddenly I could drive, I could smile, I could write. I still remember that day after my analytic session when I knew I was going to make it. I ran out, walked with confidence for the first time, hugged my dog, kissed my parents' pictures, yelled, 'I'm alive again!' I opened the blinds on my life after a year of a deathlike depression."

Davie Berman was still listed, in 1962, with the Nevada Gaming Commission as a licensed partner, with 4.5 percent shares, in the Riviera Hotel, which explained what Susan called her "trust-fund payments," which began in the early 1960s and continued throughout her college years, and into adulthood. At one point, the payments ended after a lump sum was paid to her. Susan eventually went through the money. She never disclosed to anyone what the amount was. Besides the Flamingo, Riviera, and El Cortez, Davie Berman had interest in and ran the Las Vegas Club and El Dorado.

"She appeared to have unlimited resources," UC Berkeley classmate Elizabeth Mehren said. "Unlike the rest of us, she always had money."

Even though Susan felt better emotionally, she wasn't well suited as a beat reporter and was unhappy at the *Examiner*.

The paper had hired her for entry-level beat coverage, filling in as a temporary court reporter in a musty pressroom on the fourth floor of downtown's City Hall. Friends said Susan felt insulted and underutilized. Susan lasted at the *Examiner* from 1971 to 1975.

"Her career there was not exactly meteoric," mystery writer Julie Smith told *New York* magazine. Julie was a *San Francisco Chronicle* reporter at the time. "If anything, she was not employable because she was so independent," she said. "She just couldn't work for a big company, and so she began to freelance. This is when she really came into her true flamboyance and independence. She had a great eye for the flamboyant, and she knew what would sell."

Susan had other things in mind besides the deadline grind of a daily newspaper. After four years, leaving the *San Francisco Examiner* was a mutual decision.

She began freelancing. *City* magazine, a glossy alternative publication owned by movie director Francis Ford Coppola, picked up one of Susan's articles, dreamed up by Susan after getting together with women friends in a bar one night. It was titled, "Why I Can't Get Laid in San Francisco." It caused a stir in San Francisco because it openly talked about sex, as well as the growing gay population in the Bay Area. Susan was building a name for herself in journalism circles, making a splash.

Susan's résumé was growing. In the 1970s and '80s she worked as a print and TV journalist in San Francisco and New York, first as a beat reporter for the *San Francisco Examiner*, then as a news writer-producer at San Francisco's KPIX-TV Channel 5 on the "Westinghouse Evening Show," a CBS affiliate. However, she really wanted to be a magazine journalist, so she went to work as a writer at *City* magazine, and, next, as a contributor to *New York* magazine.

Susan, often mentioned in Herb Caen's gossip columns in the *San Francisco Chronicle*, regularly lunched at the Washington Square Bar and Grill in North Beach, a restaurant affectionately known as the "Washbag." In its heyday in the 1970s and '80s the Washbag was a favorite for attorneys, advertising execs, publishing professionals, and celebrity visitors. Susan enjoyed hobnobbing with the city's movers and shakers.

Lou DeCosta said Susan "really made her mark in the Bay Area in an amazing article called 'Why I Can't Get Laid in San Francisco.' It was so bold, the nature of the article and the fact that it had been written by a woman. And the play she got with 'Why I Can't Get Laid' was huge. It made her name."

Her dean at UC Berkeley remembered the story well. "The 'Get Laid' article," Ed Bayley said, "made a big splash at the time."

"People were attracted to Susan," Bayley said. "She was lively. She seemed to like other people. She would come in to see me quite often and ask my advice. She wasn't a student of mine. I remember being sorry that she left the *Examiner* and thought she needed more newspaper experience. I remember thinking if I'd had her in my classes, I would have taught her discipline. That's what she needed. I think she probably had the idea that she was interested more in magazine than news writing right from the beginning."

Fellow UC Berkeley alum Harvey Myman also recalled Susan's reputation. "She was an interesting writer, a smart writer, I thought," Harvey Myman said. "She was never in mainstream media. She had a high profile right out of the box."

While still in San Francisco, Susan met Warren Hinckle, who today is a columnist for the *San Francisco Examiner* and based in New York City. An *Examiner* editor who said she knew them both, described the liaison as "a sexual relationship."

Susan's friend Stephen M. Silverman remembered that she'd dated her editor. "She was involved with Hinckle, as I recall," Silverman said. "Hinckle was the editor of *City* at the time she wrote her 'Laid in San Francisco' article. But she used to say she wouldn't sleep with Francis Coppola, who was the publisher. As a rule, she didn't date casually."

After the *City* article was published, while people were still talking about it, Susan drove to Los Angeles to pitch some ideas to magazines. One editor she contacted was Silverman, now with *People.com Daily* and an adjunct professor at New York's Columbia School of Journalism.

"That's how we met," Silverman told me. "I was a young editor of a magazine in Los Angeles, called *Coast* magazine. Susan had just written the cover story for *City* [magazine]. She telephoned, then came barging into the office unannounced. She introduced herself as 'the world's best writer.' She always did that."

Silverman told Susan he could give her an assignment, but she turned him down. "She never did write for *Coast* magazine," he said. "We didn't pay enough for her."

In 1976, the year after Susan left the *Examiner*, her second book, titled *Driver, Give a Soldier a Lift*, was published, this time by Putnam.

It was a novel about war in Israel and a Berkley woman's quest to find a husband.

The jacket read, "With an irrepressible wit and the sharp eyes of a keen observer, Susan Berman has written a wildly funny novel of present-day Israel—and the story of a young American girl who goes to the land of milk and honey in search of love, ending up with more than she bargained for."

The publisher, calling Susan "a fresh new talent," wrote that the book was based, in part, on Susan's personal experiences "while she lived in Israel."

The publisher was referring to Susan's summer spent in Israel when she was 18 when she met her first boyfriend. Susan also later spent nearly a year writing the book while living in Israel. She dedicated the book to her parents, a few friends, relatives, her shrink (Dr. Edward Alston), "and to the great state of Israel—may it carry on with strength forever."

Susan felt particularly connected to Israel because her father had traveled there when she was a child. "Outwardly," she wrote, "he was the first citizen of Las Vegas, promoting his town and engaging in civic and Jewish philanthropies. Inwardly he was in torment. He decided suddenly in the fall of that year [1955] to take a trip to Israel. He had never been there but had many Israeli friends from the days when he donated so much money to the Irgun.... He wanted to take me to Israel with him but said my mother would worry too much."

Susan loved the stories her father told her about Israel. "He was gone for two weeks and called me every night," Susan wrote. "He told me about Jerusalem, saying, 'I know this sounds crazy, Susie, and I never told you I believed in God, but I do now. I felt something today when I walked the streets here.'"

After publishing *Driver, Give a Soldier a Lift* Susan was getting antsy. She wanted to move to New York City, where the large national magazines were. So in 1977, Susan relocated to New York City, 2,900 miles from San Francisco on the opposite coast, where she thought she could become a "real" writer among what she considered to be the true *literati*. Susan also wanted to live in the city her father had moved to exactly 50 years earlier, in 1927, when he was just 23. He had gone to Manhattan to execute, for the mob, the kidnapping of a bootlegger. But Davie was arrested, tried, and convicted of the crime. He went to Sing Sing, a state prison in Ossining on the banks of the Hudson River just south of the farmers' dock at Sing Sing landing. Davie was released on parole after serving seven-and-a-half years of an 11-year sentence.

It was the late 1970s and Susan was living at 34 Beekman Place in Manhattan's Upper Midtown. Stephen Silverman ended up moving into the building next door to Susan's, at 32 Beekman.

"I was thinking about moving to New York," Silverman said. "She called and said there was an apartment available next to her building. It was on Beekman Place, an exclusive street in Manhattan on the East Side in the 50s. I moved into a small apartment. Susan lived in a studio. Both our apartments were tiny."

A college classmate, Harvey Myman, said he got to know Susan better in New York than he had while at UC Berkeley. He visited her on Beekman Place, with another classmate.

"By the time I knew her better, it was in New York," Harvey said. "She had written a couple of books, the one about Israel [*Driver, Give a Soldier a*

Lift], and the one about growing up in Las Vegas [*Easy Street*]. She had a bizarre fucking childhood."

He remembered Susie always hustling for new ideas. "There was a lot of chasing projects, movie this and movie that," Harvey said.

He was good friends with a fellow journalism student, Richard Zoglin, who also knew Susan at UC Berkeley.

"Richard lived in New York," Harvey said. "I was there at her Beekman Place apartment with Richard. It wasn't like Susan had said, 'I found a nice place in a nice neighborhood.' It was more like, 'I'm *going* to live on Beekman Place. *This* is the street I want to live on.' My vague sense of the apartment was that it was nicely appointed and very specifically furnished."

Susan began getting assignments from top magazine editors.

"She was writing," Stephen Silverman said. "She wrote a cover story for *New York* magazine on Bess Myerson. It upset Bess Myerson. [The magazine] titled it 'Queen Bee.'"

Susan then went to work for *Us* magazine, when it was just getting started in the early 1980s. Then CBS started a *People* magazine TV show, and "she went to work for *People*," Silverman said.

"When we were in New York, she called up a top editor," Silverman continued, "and made a luncheon date. She asked me to go with her. For a while, I was her audience. I was like the kid brother. She'd invite me to her various appointments, as a bystander. She

told the editor, 'I'm the world's best writer.' At the
end of the lunch, Susan asked the editor, 'Am I going
to write for you?' The editor very curtly said, 'I have
lots of the world's best writers right here in New
York, without you.' Susan was a steamroller.
Sometimes it worked to her advantage, and other
times it didn't. 'I can write rings around so-and-so,'
was Susan's mantra." Stephen said he remembered
the luncheon as being "exhausting. You'd go to a
restaurant and the poor waiter would get a lecture
immediately."

Back then, Silverman said he enjoyed Susan's
company. "We were pals," he said. "She lived at 34
Beekman Place. I was at 32. They were two adjoin-
ing brownstones that had been converted into studio
and one-bedroom apartments.

"They were owned by a frisky older man who
mostly liked to have sexy young women stay there.
Susan's apartment was on the ground floor, because
she hated heights. Mine was on the second. These
were really tiny apartments. They made the apartment on the 'Mary Tyler Moore' Show look like the
Taj Mahal. As I recall, my rent was $325 a month. I
think Susan's was a bit more. She had white walls
without much on them. She never used the kitchen.
She later bought a nice condo, on a low floor, in 30
Beekman Place. It was a very nice apartment,
though by then I had moved away, so I wasn't there
often."

Beekman Place, a tiny, two-block neighborhood
of luxury dwellings, is located on the fashionable

East Side of Manhattan, sandwiched between 1st Avenue and the East River, and 51st and 49th streets.

Some of the most illustrious people in society and show business at one time or another lived on that block, including Katharine Hepburn, John D. Rockefeller III, Billy Rose, Irving Berlin, James Forrestal, Katherine Cornell, David Lillienthal, Huntington Hartford, Henry Luce, to name a few.

During the time she lived there, "Susan spent money like there was no tomorrow," Silverman said. "For my 25th birthday, she took me to dinner at Elaine's. She had a trust fund. She was writing, but she didn't have a lot of money."

Even so, Susan dressed in expensive St. Laurent blouses from Saks Fifth Avenue and pricey leather boots she bought in sets of two.

She became part of the celebrated writing stable at *New York* magazine during its heyday. Also there was Nicholas Pileggi when the magazine first began publishing in 1968. He first met Susan when she started there in the late 1970s.

Still, with her career looking up, "Susan was never quite satisfied with her lot in life, always looking for something better," said Silverman. "I can't say they were halcyon days for her."

The first summer Susan lived in New York, in 1977, she received a phone call from a reporter. At the time Susan was living in a tiny one-room basement apartment with her dog, Umi, and writing for *People* magazine's TV show. A writer called her at her small ground-floor apartment. He said he was writing a book about her father. The next day she met him at Sardi's, at West 44th Street in the heart of New York City's theatre district, in Manhattan. He showed her FBI reports about her father. Page after page talked about criminal activities involving her dad.

"Did you know your father was a killer?" the reporter asked her.

Susan got up and walked out of the bar.

In September 1978, Susan's Uncle Chickie died. Only five people attended the funeral. Charles "Chickie" Berman had died, "indigent and bereft," a broken man "living in seedy motels" in Las Vegas, Susan later wrote.

That was about the time Susan befriended Danny Goldberg, now CEO of Artemis Records. "I had a PR company, called Danny Goldberg and Associates," he said. "One of my clients was the Electric Light Orchestra [band]. Susan was at *US* magazine and I was pitching her about doing a story about them. That's how we met."

She also saw Monica Bayley quite a bit, mostly for lunch, after Susan moved to New York, Ed Bayley said.

"We were in New York at the same time Susie was living in New York," he said. "She was far from the world's best writer. I'd hoped she'd get a job at a newspaper. I think she was a competent writer but not much more than that."

In fact, Susan's writing stints in New York and

her earlier reporting position at the *San Francisco Examiner* ended up being the only full-time positions she would hold in her lifetime. She chose instead to freelance.

Chapter 6
Easy Street

After fifteen years in journalism writing other people's stories, writing my father's was the toughest assignment I ever picked.
> —Susan Berman

DEATH AGAIN TOUCHED Susan's life when her Aunt Lillian died. Susan attended the tiny funeral on March 2, 1979. Only three people were there. Afterward, a friend of the family handed Susan a necklace—a medallion—her Aunt Lil had left her. Susan later bequeathed it to her best friend Bobby Durst. It was a silver dollar with an etching on one side of the Star of David and the word *Zion*. The other side said *Davie Berman*. The friend told her, "Susie, only you are left now. Maybe some day you can make the world understand that your father Davie was a good man who acted out of the most basic desire, to see his family continue and survive." Susan told her, "I intend to try."

Everyone, it seemed, was encouraging Susan to write about her Las Vegas roots, so she did. It ended up being the memoir titled *Easy Street*. It would be the highlight of her career. She would have more successes after that, but they were spread out, causing her financial difficulties off and on for the rest of her life.

It was the late 1970s and Susan began seriously delving into her father's background, which she described as his biography. It would turn out to be recognized as Susan's own memoir. *Easy Street* was officially released on October 16, 1981, and retailed for $13.95 a copy.

During her research for the book, the Superior, Wisconsin, Police Department sent Susan a mug shot of her father. She put it in her wallet and proudly showed it to everyone she knew.

An advance press release from Susan's publisher, The Dial Press, dated August 31, 1981, stated: "As a journalist, Susan Berman has a reputation for getting the 'impossible' interview. In 1977 she assigned herself the toughest investigative reporting job she had ever taken on—to find out the story her parents never wanted her to know, about her father's life as a Mob gangster. For more than two years Susan Berman traced her family history and interviewed members of the Mob to learn the truth about her father, Davie Berman. On October 16, 1981, the Dial Press will publish the most sensational personal story of the year, *Easy Street: The True Story of a Mob Family*." The book included 16 pages of black-and-white photos.

The praise for *Easy Street* was impressive. Amy

Wilentz with the *New Yorker* wrote, "A fascinating memoir." And *Publisher's Weekly* called it "A sensational story."

In 1981, an excerpt from *Easy Street* appeared as a cover story in *New York* magazine. It was, a press release said at the time, "the longest excerpt in the magazine's history." Another excerpt appeared in *Us* magazine (now *Us Weekly*) in October of the same year, coinciding with the book's release. *New York* was relatively new at that time, competing with *The New Yorker*. The glossy *New York* magazine included news features about the city as well as reporting and criticism about restaurants, the arts and entertainment in New York City.

Susan went on a month-long book tour, according to her publisher, beginning October 16, 1981, with an appearance on NBC's the *Today* show in New York, then on to Philadelphia, Boston, Washington, D.C., Baltimore, Cleveland, Chicago, Minneapolis, Seattle, San Francisco, and ending November 18 in Los Angeles. The book was received with critical acclaim. The paperback rights were sold as well. Though hardcover sales weren't as swift as expected the book received national attention.

Herbert Mitgang, both a *New York Times* correspondent and a writer for *The Montauk Fault*, reviewed *Easy Street*. He wrote, "I found it completely enthralling as a family story—so sad in its way, yet such an adventure in loyalty. The early life on a Jewish farming homestead in North Dakota especially should come as a complete revelation to many people; the search for roots there gives the book a depth beyond Las Vegas and the gangsters."

Publisher's Weekly wrote, "The author's struggle to reconcile the caring father and husband of an invalid wife—and a much-decorated war hero—with the ruthless mobster provides the real drama of this sensational story."

The 1980s were mostly good to Susan and her career. She sold the movie rights to *Easy Street* for $350,000, a good chunk of change in the early 1980s. The rights went to Polygram/Universal studios. The pair of producers working on the movie project were Alan Carr and Ray Stark, both heavy hitters in the film industry. Three years earlier, in 1978, Stark had won a Golden Globe for producing *California Suite*, and Carr had won a Globe award for *Grease*.

"I worked with her briefly," said Danny Goldberg from his New York City office. "Susan had asked me, when *Easy Street* came out, to be involved with the sale of the film rights. Although I was in the record business and not the movie business, I had some contacts there. She liked the idea that she thought she could trust me to look after her interests. She introduced me to Lynda Obst, who is a movie producer. Lynda and I were partners in the development of what maybe could have been a movie *Easy Street*. Most screenplays never get made into a movie. In that sense, like many other writers of unmade films, I think she was disappointed."

But Stephen Silverman said Susan put demands on the producers. "She insisted she had to write the screenplay," he said. "The movie fell apart. She was the queen of pushy."

Within two years, in 1983, Susan left New York City. Once again, Susan was getting antsy. Boosted financially from the sales of the movie rights and her Beekman Place apartment, she decided to move to Los Angeles to embark on a career writing screenplays in the heavily competitive field. To do that, she knew she needed to move to the West Coast, to Hollywood, where the action was. She told friends she wanted to become "a famous Hollywood screenwriter." She paid cash for a sporty new black convertible and left the Big Apple for life in the City of Angels she remembered as a child: the expensive lunches at the Brown Derby with her father and shopping sprees with her mother at the best shops Beverly Hills' Rodeo Drive had to offer.

That same year, in 1983, flush with cash, Susan took out a lease in a rental house in Beverly Hills, at 1527 Benedict Canyon Drive, the same home she would later move back into and be murdered in. In those days, it was a lovely, cheerful place. The owner, Delia "Dee" Baskin Schiffer maintained it well, according to Susan's friends.

Among the celebrated who lived on the same canyon road were Jacqueline Bisset, Elizabeth Montgomery (until her death in 1995), Mike Myers, Eddie Murphy, Martin Lawrence, Stephanie Powers, and Ann-Margret. On the darker side, actor George Reeves, best known for his role as TV's "Superman" in the 1950s, shot himself in the upstairs bedroom of his home located at 1579 Benedict Canyon Drive, across the street and just a few houses from Susan's. For years, some have said Reeves' former house was haunted and swear they've seen a ghost in the front yard wearing a "Superman" cape.

Susan loved Beverly Hills. While living there, she often shopped at Martindale's Book Store on Santa Monica Boulevard, where her father had taken her shopping for Beverly Cleary and Nancy Drew books.

Two months after Susan's arrival in L.A., while standing in the script registration line at the Writers Guild office, she met Mister Margulies. ("Yes, that was his name," Susan wrote in *Lady Las Vegas*.) He was 25 and a starving poet. Susan was 38 and fresh off of a book tour. "I know you," he told her. In *Easy Street*, Susan wrote that Mister recognized her from her author photos on the jacket of her books. Mister's father, Jay Margulies, who once worked for Susan's dad, had her books. "He loved your dad," Mister told Susan. In fact, he said, according to Susan's account in *Lady Las Vegas*, "My Hebrew name is David Abraham. I was named for your dad. I'm from Vegas."

"*You're* from Vegas?" Susan responded, incredulously. Like Susan, Mister's childhood was spent in the Mohave Desert.

"Yeah, I'm from Vegas, and I'm a writer," he said. She fell instantly in love. Susan later wrote that she married him "for the brilliant, loving, unique person he was."

Ruthie Bartnof, who was best friends with Mister's mother until her death in 2001, said, "Their fathers were close, but Susan and Mister had never met [as children], so it was amazing that they met by accident in line at the Writers Guild."

At the time of that first meeting, Susan was wearing a large gold necklace and pendant with the words "Easy Street" spelled out. Her friend Elizabeth Mehren remembered it well. "It was too big," she said of the piece of jewelry.

Just before her wedding, Susan had dinner with Elizabeth.

"There was always a project she had going about Las Vegas," Elizabeth Mehren said. "It was so pathetic. I don't know if she was trying to answer the questions to her life or whether she genuinely was interested in what she was doing. I remember thinking, *This is a woman who made a career out of being the orphaned daughter of the Jewish mobster from Las Vegas.* She was stuck there."

"She never could shirk that part of her life," Elizabeth continued. "She basically exploited it. And it's all just an illusion. She couldn't give any of it up, right down to the little-girl hairdo."

Rilo Weisner grew up in the desert with Mister and his sister Candace. "I knew Mister when he was a kid," Rilo said from her Las Vegas home. "His sister Candy and I were the same age. He was always her little brother to me. We went to Sunday school together." They graduated from high school in 1969, with Mister a year behind them.

"Mister and Susan had similar backgrounds," Rilo said. "Jay [Mister's father] ran the gift shop at the Riviera, and Mister was always going to the Strip. He was used to being treated like he was Las Vegas royalty, similar to Susan. My mother and his mother were very close friends.

"He was an observer. There was a sense of mystery about him, like he had a secret. But he was witty and bright."

In June 1984, Susan and Mister married. Susan paid for a lavish wedding at the elegant Hotel Bel-Air, a red-tiled Mediterranean villa nestled on 11-acre park-like grounds and gardens. Susan ordered expensive ice swans, like the ones her father once regularly ordered for the Flamingo Hotel. The wedding was held outside, near the hotel's Swan Lake. Susan asked Bobby Durst to walk her down the aisle. Without hesitation, he agreed. Bobby had evolved from the brother Susan never had to a father figure. With Susan on his arm, he walked her down the aisle and gave her away. At the reception, movie producer Robert Evans delivered the toast. Susan could not have been prouder.

The hotel was the same one Susan's cousin Raleigh Padveen had been married in some 30-odd years earlier. Raleigh was Davie Berman's favorite niece. Susan remembered how happy her father had been at Raleigh's wedding. "He stood for hours talking to friends and relatives as he watched the swans swim in the outdoor pond," Susan wrote in *Easy Street*. It was as if, with her own wedding, which cost her a bundle, Susan was trying to get close to her father, to feel at home once again, by replicating her cousin's blissful ceremony.

Mister moved into Susan's rented Benedict Canyon house. "There was love in the house," Susan's friend Kim Lankford told *New York* magazine. "They were crazy about each other."

Elizabeth Mehren said Susan tried to set her up on a date for the wedding with one of the Durst brothers.

"I was living in Santa Monica and I remember having dinner with her one night at the old restaurant on Wilshire called the Bicycle [Shop] Cafe," Elizabeth said. "At some point, she told me she was dating and she had fallen in love with this man. He was younger than she was, by a lot. She told me his name. Mister Margulies. I asked her, 'Well, what do you call him for short?' She looked at me, mystified, and said, 'Mister.' She wanted to invite me to her wedding at the Hotel Bel-Air. She wanted to set me up with her friend. She wanted me to sit at the table with one of the Dursts, either Bobby or Doug. I just dimly remember 'Bobby' as being part of the discussion. I didn't go to the wedding because I was in the process of being swept off my feet by another man."

That was the last time Elizabeth heard from Susan.

Shortly after their marriage, Susan chose to live in Brentwood—as was her habit of living amidst and hobnobbing with the elite. Brentwood was, and still is, another posh neighborhood in the west end of Los Angeles, comprised of mostly mansions for the well-to-do. Susan bought a home in the exclusive community, located just off Sunset Boulevard, at 12030 Coyne Street, around the corner from the Bundy Drive townhouse Nicole Brown Simpson would live and die in.

But even a beautiful home couldn't give Susan the happiness she was seeking, or save her marriage. Her relationship with Mister was unraveled quickly. Susan was heartbroken.

Susan and Mister's marriage lasted about seven months. She called friends, crying and saying, "It's over. He's been doing drugs again and he's been abusing me."

Mister had fallen back into his drug habit.

Susan knew when she married Mister that he'd done heroin, but she thought he'd quit. Susan wasn't a user, friends said. "Her friends were very druggy, but she wasn't," Stephen Silverman recalled. "[And] she just didn't like alcohol, although it might also have had something to do with her allergy to wheat."

Two years after Susan met her husband, and after the couple had already divorced, Mister, at age 27, died of a self-induced drug overdose. Susan wrote in *Lady Las Vegas* that Mister was "on the brink of Hollywood success as a screenwriter" when he died. At the time, Susan and Mister were working at reconciliation. Following his death, Susan had an emotional breakdown. She began seeing a psychic to help her through her depression. She developed allergies and more phobias. The losses in her life were almost too much for Susan to bear. First, she lost her father, then her mother, her Uncle Chickie and Aunt Lil, and, finally, Mister Margulies. Even though they were divorced, Susan's friends described Mister as "the love of her life."

After Mister's death, Susan stayed in touch with his mother, Harriet Margulies, who died in September 2001. "Susan was very close to Harriet," Ruthie Bartnof said. "She remained in touch with her, and Harriett felt as though Susan was part of Mister. Susan was broken up about his death. Her whole life was so tragic."

But amidst the tragedy and sorrow in her life, Ruthie noted that "it was so much fun being with her. She was *really* fun. She knew everybody. She had a way about her. She had her own groupies, people who loved being around her. Even with the sadness, she had a great sense of humor. Her heartache was really that of an abandoned child."

To help her work through her grief in losing Mister, Susan eventually penned an unpublished biography about him.

"I have some of her original manuscripts," Ruthie Bartnof said. "She wrote a manuscript about Mister. I read it, but I don't know what Susan did with it."

About Mister's death, Susan later wrote in *Lady Las Vegas*, "Mister didn't make it out of Vegas alive.... Did he meet the doom meant for me? Is there a curse on Vegas parents and their children?"

Chapter 7

Bobby Durst

AS A YOUNG MAN, Robert Alan Durst had it all—monied family, good grades, handsome looks, charisma. He was raised in the well-to-do Westchester suburb of Scarsdale, New York. The children Bobby grew up with were the sons and daughters of some of the wealthiest and most influential families in the country. Their parents were either corporate bigwigs or heavy-duty lawyers, and prominent Wall Street bankers; their mothers were socialites. Their children led comfortable and sheltered existences.

Even so, something went terribly wrong with Bobby. He appeared to have gone mad. That madness led him to be on the lam for more than two months, a fugitive of justice, only to be caught, dumbfounding those who knew him.

As a younger man, he was handsomer, hobnobbing about town with the likes of Jackie Onassis and

Mia Farrow. He had an affair with Mia's sister, Prudence Farrow. Prudence's beauty was the inspiration for the Beatles song "Dear Prudence."

Robert Durst, nicknamed Bobby, was the oldest of three children and the son of New York real estate developer Seymour B. Durst, patriarch of a family real estate empire worth billions. The senior Durst was once one of New York City's richest and most powerful real estate developers who built a half dozen office buildings on Third Avenue in Manhattan after World War II. He died in 1995. The name Seymour Durst often can be found alongside other notable New York developers such as Stanley Stahl, Sol Goldman, and Harry Helmsley. The elder Durst was also noted for his frequent small ads on the front page of the *New York Times* bemoaning the national debt and expressing his views on other political matters. The senior Durst paid for the widely recognized National Debt Clock on New York's Avenue of the Americas. City University of New York dedicated a library to him. The library, in the school's graduate center, contains Seymour's extensive collection of New York historical books and memorabilia. The collection once filled every inch of Seymour's palatial East Side town house, including books stuffed in his refrigerator.

Seymour was the son of Joseph Durst, a Jewish immigrant from Poland. After 13 years working in the garment district, Joseph had saved enough money to buy a Midtown Manhattan office building. The purchase became the cornerstone of the Durst family's real estate empire. Joseph's elder son Seymour eventually took over the helm of the Durst Organization. Seymour and his wife Bernice had four children. Robert was their eldest son, with brothers Douglas and Thomas, and sister Wendy.

As his business prospered, Seymour moved his family to Scarsdale, a tiny suburb with architecture reminiscent of its English roots.

A bustling ritzy village of mostly single-family estate homes worth millions, Scarsdale offered Bobby an enviable quality of life in one of New York's wealthiest real-estate families. Born in 1943, he grew up on Hampton Road and attended Scarsdale High, from where he graduated in 1961. Like Susan Berman's background, it was a childhood of privilege.

But Bobby's comfortable early years were forever marred by tragedy when, on a rainy autumn night in 1950 when Bobby was seven, his mother, dressed in a nightgown, climbed out of a second-story bedroom window and onto the slippery roof of their suburban Westchester stone mansion and fell to her death. She either fell or jumped from the rain-slick roof of the mansion, landing on the driveway. Bobby was the only one of the Durst children to witness his mother's tragic ending. Newspaper accounts at the time stated that Bernice, 32, became disoriented after an overdose of asthma medication. Privately, family members acknowledged that Bernice committed suicide. Bobby was stoic about his mother's death, at least on the surface. But he underwent counseling for bouts of depression and angry rivalry battles with his younger brother Douglas.

As time passed, Bobby appeared to develop emotionally into a normal teenager and looked as if he had recovered from the tragedy. As a teenager, he was relatively calm by nature and an undistinguished student. Bobby's family and friends described him as quiet, shy, and a loner—that is, unless you got to know him. That's when his loud and often crude antics and dry sense of humor kicked in.

Richard Guggenheimer, a high school classmate, knew Bobby's brother Doug and his cousin Peter, but could barely recall the reserved Bobby, just a year ahead of him. And Dorothy Ciner, whose name and identity Bobby later used, was in the same class but didn't know him. He left little in the way of lasting impressions. Bobby's charisma developed later, during his university years. The 1961 Scarsdale High yearbook showed a single photo of Robert and no mention of extracurricular school activities.

After high school, he went on to college at Lehigh University, a private institution, in Bethlehem, Pennsylvania, in a tree-lined city of 45,000. His college education began in fall 1961 and lasted through to spring 1965—a hundred miles from the hubbub of New York City, where the family business was. The registrar's office shows that Bobby Durst graduated on Monday, June 14, 1965, with a bachelor of science degree in business administration and a declared major in economics. In the summer and after college, Bobby worked on and off for his father at the Durst Organization in Manhattan.

In September 1967, Bobby enrolled in graduate school at the University of California at Los Angeles, where he met Susan Berman. Bobby's scholastic emphasis was again on economics. He left UCLA, according to the registrar's records, in March 1968 without earning a graduate degree. The next year, Bobby Durst went back to work for his father, in Manhattan, where he would meet his future wife, Kathleen McCormack, two years later.

Kathleen had recently moved to the city from her home in New Hyde Park, New York, renting an apartment in a building owned by Durst's family. That's when Bobby and Kathie met and started dating. It was a whirlwind romance; they moved in together almost immediately, after just two dates. They soon relocated to rural Vermont. where they opened a natural health food store called All Good Things. *To hell with business and economics*, Bobby is said to have remarked.

They were a striking couple, he with his good looks, athletic body, and charm, and she with her pretty face, caring disposition, and pleasant personality. He had a dry sense of humor; she was smart, sweet, and funny. Seymour Durst was disappointed that his son, with his economics background, chose instead to run a health food store. At the urging of the senior Durst, Bobby and Kathie returned to New York in 1973, where they married. They appeared, on the outside, to be a charmed couple.

Although Bobby joined his father and brother Douglas in the family business, he resisted the trappings of the upper-class, preferring, instead, to drive an old Volkswagen Beetle, wear casual hippie-like attire, and sport a goatee.

Conversely, his wife Kathie loved the bright lights of New York City and the good life afforded by Bobby's family fortune.

"It was as though Cinderella had married Prince Charming," Kathie's older brother, Jim McCormack, told *New York* magazine. "He had the resources to do the things she had dreamed of doing. Robert was shy—not exactly antisocial but reluctant to enter into conversations. Kathie was the exact opposite—vivacious, witty, ready to enjoy life. She brought out the best in him."

Still, their life together was far from perfect. In spite of their wealth, Kathie drove an old Mercedes and complained that Bobby was too cheap to buy her a new one. She told friends she was unhappy with what she termed "living below our means." She was also disappointed that Bobby did not want children. In perhaps the most telling statement Kathie confided to friends was that Bobby was still deeply disturbed by his mother's death. It was an explanation, in large part, as to why Bobby appeared to have lost touch with reality as an adult.

Kathie decided to pursue a career in medicine, first gaining a nursing degree from Western Connecticut State University in Danbury. During the school week, Kathie stayed at their country waterfront cottage on Lake Truesdale in the Westchester County village of South Salem, while Robert remained in Manhattan, at their penthouse on the Upper West Side, at 76th Avenue and Riverside Drive. To escape New York City's annual wave of summer heat and high humidity, the privileged few find refuge in rural retreats. Bobby and Kathie were among the elite with the means to do so. On weekends Bobby was there with his wife. They often invited their friends to visit the lakefront property.

"Kathie was very much in love with Bobby when I met her," said Gilberta Najamy, today a women's counselor who became Kathie's friend after meeting her in 1976 while they were undergraduate classmates at Western Connecticut. "From Monday until Friday she would wait by the phone for him to call."

Later, after Kathie was admitted to the Albert Einstein School of Medicine in the Bronx, Najamy and other friends visited the city on weekends to party with Kathie.

Using Bobby's connections, the group got reservations at expensive restaurants and trendy nightclubs like Studio 54 and Xenon. Sometimes Bobby accompanied them, but he seldom seemed to enjoy it.

"Bobby was not thrilled with her circle of friends," Najamy said. "I think he suspected that we were telling her that she didn't need him or his money, which we were."

Bobby became "possessive and abusive," Najamy

recalled, sometimes taking his anger out on bystanders. At the Durst's penthouse after a night of clubbing, Bobby assaulted one of Najamy's friends, a photographer named Peter Schwartz, because Schwartz was too slow to move when Durst ordered everyone out of the apartment. And Kathie's brother Jim McCormack told friends he once saw Bobby grab his sister by the hair and jerk her off the sofa at their mother's home in New Hyde Park.

If Kathleen Durst were alive today, she'd be 49 years old. The last night she was seen, Kathie had been at Gilberta Najamy's Connecticut house, attending a party. Bobby had called the house several times, ordering Kathie to return home.

Kathie left, but not before she told Gilberta, "If anything happens to me, Bobby did it." Kathie had been drinking that night, but left for home anyway, alone, at about 7:30 p.m. Drugs and liquor were reportedly free-flowing among the reveling crowd, and there were reports that Kathie took drugs socially.

Eleanor Schwank told "ABC News" that Kathie said something similar to her and that she was afraid of her husband. Schwank quoted Kathie as saying, "If anything ever happens to me, don't let Bobby get away with it."

Bobby first said Kathie went home to their South Salem cottage, then changed his story and said she went directly to their Manhattan penthouse because she had to attend classes, at Albert Einstein School of Medicine, on Monday. Bobby admitted to police that the couple had fought, but said it was an argument on the phone.

Five days after his wife's disappearance, on Friday, February 5, 1982, Robert Durst walked into the New York Police Department's 20th Precinct, a busy office at 120 West 82nd Street on Manhattan's Upper West Side. The precinct covers 1.1 dense square miles and includes in its jurisdiction the American Museum of National History, American Museum of Folk Art, Manhattan Children's Museum, Julliard School of Performing Arts, and New York Historical Society. Bobby officially filed a missing persons report, telling officers he didn't know where his wife was and that he had nothing to do with her disappearance. Bobby's demeanor, whether it was sad, subdued, stoic, or unemotional, wasn't noted in the police report.

Bobby told officers he dropped off Kathie at the Katonah train station on January 31, 1982, after she came home from a party. They'd had an argument about her being out late, he told NYPD Detective Michael Struk. He told the detective that 45 minutes after his wife arrived, she left with a suitcase for Manhattan. He said he put his wife on the 9:17 PM train in Katonah, Westchester County, near the couple's South Salem home, bound for their Upper West Side apartment. Durst told police he spoke with Kathie on the phone from home, just after 11 o'clock that night, after she arrived at their penthouse.

Three witnesses backed up Bobby's account of

that evening. The dean of the medical college said he received a call from Kathie the following morning saying she wouldn't be in class. An elevator operator said he saw Kathie in the Manhattan apartment building. And the building super said he saw her on the street the next morning.

Bobby made headlines a week later when the New York *Daily News* ran a front-page story with Bobby's offer of $100,000 for information about Kathie's disappearance. Police said that no real leads came out of the reward money.

Then, Durst's story changed when Susan Berman became his unofficial spokeswoman. Susan, who already loved Bobby like he was family, took to the role of spokesperson easily. It was a natural one for Susan, whose writing career took off with *Easy Street,* the book that successfully portrayed Davie Berman the loving father contrasting his public image as a ruthless gangster.

Through Susan, Bobby told police and reporters that instead of calling Kathie from the South Salem house, he'd made the call from a pay phone while out walking his dog Igor. The problem with that version, however, was that the nearest public telephone was miles away, and it was a cold night, with slushy snow on the ground.

That's why some believed Kathleen Durst didn't make it out of Westchester alive that night.

After Bobby Durst told police his wife was missing, he walked out of the police bureau a free man. It was the last time Bobby Durst cooperated with police about his missing wife.

NYPD issued a missing persons bulletin on Kathie Durst. Years later, with the advent of the Internet, the bulletin was posted on NYPD's Web site, stating that it was from the Long Term Cases. A photo ran with it. (NYPD misspelled Kathie Durst's first name, spelling it "Kathy"). The release stated:

MISSING PERSON: Kathy Durst
DESCRIPTION
At Time of Disappearance:
Sex: Female
Race: White
Age: 29

Last seen: On January 31, 1982, in Manhattan, New York, within the confines of the 20th Precinct.

If you know the whereabouts or can add to the circumstances of a person classified as missing, please notify the Missing Persons Squad at 1-646-610-6914. Favor de notificar a Missing Persons Squad 1-646-610-6914.

Based on eyewitness accounts, investigators initially believed Kathie Durst arrived safely in Manhattan and focused their search there. But later, they came to believe the witnesses who reported seeing or hearing from Kathie were either mistaken or deceived. Still, the case was at a standstill.

With Kathie Durst's 1982 disappearance, Bobby simply stopped talking about his wife. He immersed himself in the family business. He managed Durst properties, buying and selling new ones and drumming up additional business.

Then, at a Christmas party in 1988 at the

Rainbow Room, Bobby met real estate agent Debrah Charatan. He dated her off and on for 12 years.

In 1990, Durst published paid notices of his pending divorce to his wife Kathleen in a Westchester County weekly newspaper as part of a legal requirement that he attempt to notify his missing spouse. He didn't tell anyone about his divorce. Kathie's family wouldn't learn about it for another decade.

Bobby continued to work hard for the Durst Organization. But in a huge blow to Bobby's future—and ego—the aging Seymour Durst decided on a successor: Douglas Durst. When Bobby heard the news that his younger brother was taking over the family business, he walked out of his office, never to return. He never spoke to his family again, only speaking to his sister Wendy and a bevy of family attorneys.

Today, the Durst empire owns eleven prominent skyscrapers, including buildings that house the headquarters of Pfizer and AOL Time Warner. The family business, now run by Douglas, is reportedly worth $2 billion.

Chapter 8
Writing About Las Vegas

I think it will always be a small town to me, for how can we separate our childhood's from our hometowns?

—Susan Berman
from *Lady Las Vegas*

SUSAN CONTINUED her writing career while acting as her best friend Bobby's liaison to the police and media.

"I was born to write," Susan Berman once said in an interview. "I handicapped the Academy Awards for my block when I was nine."

Susan seemed to always fall back on her Las Vegas background. Whether it was part nostalgia, part searching for her roots, part cashing in on her town, or all of the above, Las Vegas held an allure for her, held her at bay. People have always been curious about the desert oasis and its past, so throughout her writing career, Susan wrote about the town she felt she knew best and had grown up in.

Included in the February 1998 issue of *Las Vegas Life*, a glossy magazine started a year earlier by the owners of the *Las Vegas Sun*. Susan had allowed an excerpt of *Easy Street* to be published in the magazine as an article titled "Growing Up On Easy Street." Then, in July of the same year, the magazine published another article by Susan, titled "The Heat: Memoirs of an Earlier Vegas." The pieces were excerpted from her original memoir from 17 years earlier.

Susan told friends it was "beneath" her to write for such a small publication. To be sure, the local magazine didn't pay the $2- to $4-per-word rate the national magazine writers were getting—she was lucky if she was paid $150 for each piece. But Susan, at that point, was broke and almost desperate for money. So when she was contacted to write something for *Las Vegas Life*, Susan acquiesced.

Mister Margulies's best friend, Kevin Bartnof, who grew up with Mister in Las Vegas, also wrote a piece for *Las Vegas Life*, published in its July 1998 issue. After Mister's death, Susan and Kevin became good friends. "She and Kevin were so close," said Kevin's mother Ruthie. "They weren't romantically inclined at all. They were like brother and sister. She would help him with his writing. He was upset about her death, then six months later Kevin died."

Susan helped Kevin with his *Las Vegas Life* piece, Ruthie said. He wrote about his search, as a teenager, for Elvis Presley in Las Vegas. "So much time has passed," Kevin, then a foley artist in Hollywood, wrote. "My friend Mister died eleven years ago in January. Every day something reminds me of him.... I wound up in Los Angeles, doing sound effects for the movies—honest work, a heck of a paper route.

"But on an unseasonably cool night, I realize that the collection of Elvis paraphernalia atop my fireplace is not merely a shrine to the King of Rock 'n' Roll, but an acknowledgment of youth and friendship, a memorial to our adolescent journey, a time that's forever lost, but not forgotten."

Susan, too, was a big Elvis fan. When she was a young girl, Elvis was in town. "Of course I was crazy about Elvis Presley," Susan said in her A&E network documentary *The Real Las Vegas*. "I was somewhere with my dad and I knew that Elvis Presley was playing the hotel, and I said, 'You know, if you're so important, have Elvis Presley sing "Happy Birthday" to me,' and he did. That was something." He signed a photograph and gave it to Susan. It read, "To Susan, Best wishes, Elvis." It was dated 1957, for Susan's 12th birthday.

Six months after Susan was killed, Kevin, on June 30, 2001, suffered from a massive heart attack and died.

Susan had wanted to be as successful as Shana Alexander, a veteran journalist and literary author living in New York, whom she greatly admired. Unfortunately, Susan's successes with her early writings were short-lived.

"She so wanted to make it big," said Stephen M. Silverman, a fellow writer who has penned nine books. "But she was not big. She would have liked to have been Shana Alexander, but she never came close. Her writing was too uneven. Besides *New York* [magazine], she also wrote for the *Times*, though she was ticked off that all they asked her to do was a story on picnic baskets for their recently launched food section. She thought picnic baskets were beneath her."

Susan never did make it *really* big. It would be her greatest disappointment.

"She wanted recognition," Ruthie Bartnof said. "Hers was a pursuit of recognition for her writing, for her talents. I think she wanted that success so badly."

Susan's biggest successes came when she parlayed her Las Vegas background into writing projects. But she turned away work when she felt it didn't pay enough, leaving long periods between assignments and projects—and paychecks.

Still, in December 1982, Bantam Books released a paperback edition of *Easy Street*. Sales initially were swift, and life was going well for Susan. It was an important book for her, especially after the failed movie deal of the same title.

Around 1987 Susan met Paul Kaufman, the man her friends said was her last real boyfriend. He was a financial adviser with Hollywood aspirations and a single father with two teenaged children. Kaufman and his kids moved into Susan Berman's Brentwood home, just around the corner from the town house where Nicole Brown Simpson and Ron

Goldman were killed. And, for a while anyway, he made her happy. Susan adored Kaufman's children, Mella and Sareb, 24 and 26 at the time of Susan's death. They considered Susan their mother. "She held my hand through everything difficult in life," Sareb, who works in the recording business, told *New York* magazine. "She was the only person who was always on my side and never judged me."

Her relationship with Paul ended in 1992, when Susan ran out of money. Susan and Paul had begun working on a Broadway musical based on the Dreyfus affair, about an anti-Semitic case in 19th century France. Susan sunk money from her assets into the new project. It failed. And so did their relationship.

In 1992, the bank foreclosed on Susan's Brentwood home and she was forced to file for bankruptcy. The financial difficulties and the failure of the play undid their relationship. They split up. Mella stayed with Susan; Sareb moved in with Paul.

Susan was broke. A friend offered her use of a condo near the Sunset Strip, at 2121 Avenue of the Stars, also a street famous for its celebrity residents, including Norman Lear, television producer, writer, and director. Susan and Mella lived there for five years, rent free.

"Being a mother to these kids was one of the proudest and most satisfying things in her life," Rich Markey told a reporter.

Susan began writing mysteries and short stories to pay her expenses and Mella's private-school tuition. She and Mella also co-wrote an unpublished manuscript, titled *Never a Mother, Never a Daughter*.

Susan had desperately wanted children of her own; at one point, she even discussed with her friends about asking Bobby Durst to father a child with her. After Mella and Sareb moved with their father to Susan's, she no longer talked about it. She had the children she'd longed for.

At some point during her years in L.A., Susan lived in West Hollywood in The Park Wellington apartment building, complete with a doorman 24 hours a day.

Once she was back on her feet again, Susan telephoned her former landlady Dee Schiffer and asked if she could move back into the Benedict Canyon Drive house. The rented house was about to be vacant so Dee said, "Okay." In 1998, Susan moved back to the house where she ultimately was murdered.

The biggest thing to come out of that period was Susan's return to writing about Las Vegas. She always returned to what she knew best—the Las Vegas scene—as fodder for her writing.

It meant a book deal and an A&E network special called *The Real Las Vegas*. It brought her new acclaim and fresh cash (and showed, perhaps, a lack of caution, since she'd once told Julie Smith that, after *Easy Street*, she'd been warned, *Don't ever mess with us again*).

The second half of the 1990s were a financial roller coaster for Susan. Although she landed another book deal, she had trouble getting contracts for her other projects. But she still lived in Beverly Hills, struggling while living among the rich.

Susan could have gone out and gotten a full-time job. But because of her early opulent background, she felt entitled to money without having to struggle to make a day-to-day living. Instead, she hit up friends for loans. The lifestyle Susan's father had lavished on her had spoiled her.

Las Vegas, Susan had written, "taught me always to eat out, to stay only in the best hotels, and to appreciate a good sense of humor." She considered Las Vegas her hometown. But she didn't have anywhere to go while there. Her parents were dead. She was an only child. Her friends were her family now. She couldn't go home, back to her roots in Las Vegas, so Susan wrote about her desert home.

Susan had "arrived with much fanfare, great talent, and then for years and years and years, nothing happened," Julie Smith told *New York* magazine. "She went through all her money from the movie sale and the book royalties."

Her childhood friend, Bob Miller, talked about her writings. "She had good credentials," he said. "She was a small child when she left, but she certainly touched the right bases when she came back. We discussed on the phone several times who she needed to talk to, what Las Vegas had become. I read her books. We talked about getting together sometime to reminisce about what it was like when we were children. That never happened. I thought she had an interesting writing style. She was nostalgic. In context of her earlier book *Easy Street*, it was nostalgia. She had a rivalry with her background."

In August 1995, an excerpt of *Easy Street* was included in *Literary Las Vegas: The Best Writing About America's Most Fabulous City*, a 358-page paperback edited by Mike Tronnes with an introduction by Nick Tosches. It was a break for Susan and gave her more notoriety and approval for her writing. She was considered an expert on 1950s Las Vegas. It also gave her a small royalty check.

A. J. Liebling with *Booklist* gave the book a glowing review. He wrote, "The essays and short stories in this collection reveal the glitz and history of a city that has gone from 'mobster and starlet hideaway, to haven of sin and vice, to its present incarnation as low-roller heaven' and still remains the marriage capital of the U.S. As the editor notes, 'Who else but Las Vegas would make the A-bomb a picnic? An honest-to-God picnic.' Believe it or not, tourists would travel to a local hilltop, with lunches provided by the casinos, to view the test blasting of the atomic bombs. There is plenty of more fascinating reading for those who love, hate, or never even thought much about this city. There are tales of lounge lizards, millionaires, showgirls, gangsters, gamblers, and businessmen from writers such as Joan Didion, Noel Coward, Hunter S. Thompson...."

Ingram Books called it "a humorous, anecdotal history of Las Vegas" that "chronicles the days of glitter gulch to the building of modern resorts."

Literary Las Vegas was touted by the publisher as offering views "through the eyes of some of America's best writers." Excerpted were Susan's recollections of her father teaching her math by giving her a slot machine to play with and the Sabbath meals that her grandmother prepared for her father's Jewish gangster associates.

Susan was in good company. Twenty-five pieces were in the book with hers, including a 1964 article which Tom Wolf wrote for *Esquire*, an excerpt from Hunter S. Thompson's classic *Fear and Loathing in Las Vegas*, a diary of Noel Coward's Las Vegas experiences, and a 1952 article from the *New Yorker* about atomic bomb testing when rooftop parties welcomed the flashes of light in the desert.

Then, in another high-profile opportunity for Susan, on September 19, 1997, "This American Life," from WBEC Chicago's Public Radio International, aired a piece titled "The Mob," which featured Susan Berman in Act II. The station titled it "Mob Daughter."

The commentator, Alec Wilkinson, explained Susan's role like this: "So let's say your father is a big-time gangster. And, like the man in the *Godfather* movies, actually *does* try to protect you from ever knowing what exactly he does for a living. What happens when you find out? Well, Susan Berman's father died of natural causes when she was 12. Her mother died a year later, and the first time anyone directly told Susan about her father's underworld ties was when she was in college.

Another student told her about this new book that talked about what her father really did for a living."

Others interviewed were Danny Toro, a member of a Chicago street gang, Teresa Dalessio, daughter of a New York Mafia family, New York underworld reporter Jerry Capesi, and Wilkinson of *The New Yorker*.

Wilkinson described Susan's seven-minute reading and 13-minute comments as "Susan Berman's memories of Jewish gangsters and their gangster-style Jewish mothers." Then, he said, after a break, "Act Two. Mobster Daughter. Susan Berman, author of the memoir *Easy Street*, reads from her book about her father Davie Berman, a Jewish gangster and one of the men—with Meyer Lansky and Bugsy Siegel—who created modern Las Vegas. Act Two continues after the break. More from Susan Berman on her father, who was a coldhearted mobster by day and a devoted family man at night, just like gangsters in movies like *The Godfather*."

Susan explained, on the air, how she reacted when she learned that her father was a high-ranking member of the Jewish mob: "I rushed to Martindale's book store in Beverly Hills, no longer existent. And, you know, quickly found this book the *Green Felt Jungle*. There was a huge display of them and I quickly looked at the index, "Davie Berman." And it did, it had a whole chapter on the Flamingo Hotel and Ben Siegel's death, and it said that after Ben Siegel was dead, that Davie Berman, and in parentheses, 'who could kill a man with one hand behind his back,' and a little later in the chapter it said that he had been wounded in a shootout with an FBI man in Central Park and done 11 years in Sing Sing, and then it went on to talk about his other partners. Well, I started to throw up in the book store, I was so shocked. Literally. How gross, right? It was just a visceral reaction, you know? I couldn't believe it. And, of course, I didn't think it was true."

The commentator continued. "She worked so hard at believing this wasn't true," he said, "that eventually she forgot this ever happened. Years later, she was a reporter for the *San Francisco Examiner* and interviewed Jimmy Hoffa just a month before he vanished. He and his men all knew her dad. One of them said, 'He was much smarter than the guys running the Outfit now.' And, *still*, she didn't want to believe her dad was with the mob. Finally, when someone showed her her father's files, finally then, reluctantly, she believed."

In fact, authors Ed Reid and Ovid Demaris, in *Green Felt Jungle*, described Susan's father as "an ex-con who served time in Sing Sing for kidnapping and a former Siegel thug who was soon to become the muscle behind Greenbaum." Dave Berman is referenced five times in the book, which today is a classic.

In 1996 Morrow/Avon publishers released Susan Berman's *Fly Away Home*, a paperback novel about a young woman's search for her missing sister. The culprit, it turned out, was in the heroine's midst: the boyfriend of her character's missing sister.

The last lines of Susan's book, although fiction, read: "If I can't take anything positive from the lives of my parents, maybe I can find something positive in the way I've handled the revelations. They say life is a gift. I may soon be ready to open it."

In her dedication, Susan included a group of friends. Bobby's name topped the list. "This book is dedicated with love and gratitude," Susan wrote, "to my treasured friends with whom I have been fortunate to share life's journey: Bobby Durst, Nina Feinberg, Danny Goldberg, Judith Sherwood Hafeman, Susie [Amateau] Harmon, Sheila Jaffe Krimshtein, Florean Mader, Laraine Newman, Ainslie Pryor, Bede Roberts, Julie Smith."

On the cover of the book was a short review by Julie Smith, author of the acclaimed *House of Blues*. The review read, "A fast, sexy read.... Susan Berman is a terrific new writer on the suspense scene." The book, however, did not stay in print more than a couple of years. It was another huge disappointment for Susan. Still, she persevered. She kept pitching projects, hoping that one would bring her the wealth she was seeking.

In 1996, Susan co-produced *The Las Vegas Story*, a documentary for A&E that brought her recognition from her colleagues. In the documentary, the one for which Susan received a Writers Guild of America nomination, she delved into the shady beginnings of Sin City.

That same year, while doing research in Las Vegas for the A&E documentary, Susan attended the Golden Nugget's 50th anniversary party. "Steve Wynn knows how to throw a party," Susan later wrote. Wynn publicly announced Susan's presence and introduced her as "Davie Berman's daughter." Old-timers approached Susan and told her that her dad was "a great guy."

Then, at the A&E premier, held Thursday, November 14, 1996, at Planet Hollywood in Beverly Hills, Susan signed a copy of *Lady Las Vegas* for the state of Nevada's archives. Guy Rocha, archivist and historian for the state and a consultant on *The Real Las Vegas* series, handed Susan the copy. Susan wrote, "To my hometown Lady Las Vegas. I have the utmost respect for you. You're the greatest hometown in the world. I'm 51 & you're 91. We face the millennium together. Love, Susan Berman."

Rocha later commented, "There is some real irony here, particularly if you believe that the millennium actually began in 2001."

The blurb for the series went like this: "It's a city that's larger than life. A city without limits. A glittering mecca of excess and forbidden desires. Discover the fascinating story of this fabled destination and the people who created it. From the mobsters who made Vegas into their version of the American Dream to the tycoons of today's family mega-resorts, this is the ultimate insider's tour of America's neon oasis. Illuminating interviews with luminaries like Alan King, Wayne Newton and Debbie Reynolds, writer Nick Pileggi, entrepreneur Steve Wynn and Howard Hughes frontman Robert

Maheu offer a unique, unvarnished look at the fabled city, while never-before-seen footage opens a window to its tumultuous past. Tour the incredible casinos of the world-famous strip and even get tips on how to beat the odds! Bonus: With any order of *The Real Las Vegas*, receive the companion hardcover book by author and series writer Susan Berman, daughter of Bugsy Siegel's partner Davie Berman."

Lady Las Vegas's publisher, TV Books, included on the book jacket, "Berman takes her memories, her candor, and pain and revisits the town where the American dream is chased, found and lost a thousand times a day. Las Vegas is Susan Berman's hometown.... Berman grew up alongside Las Vegas, maturing with the city."

More and more, Susan was being called upon as an expert on Vegas's early mob days, mostly because she was Davie Berman's daughter, but also because she'd carved out a niche for herself as well. An interview with Susan about Bugsy Siegel for "Mysteries & Scandals," hosted by A.J. Benza for E!, first aired April 27, 1998. Susan talked about her father and how he and his partners took over the operation of the Flamingo Hotel immediately following Bugsy Siegel's murder.

Even Susan's own novels eerily resembled her life. *Spiderweb*, a paperback released in 1997 by Avon, seemed loosely based on her own experiences. Amazon.com's description read: "Few crime novelists come to their craft with more impressive credentials than Susan Berman, who grew up in a

Mafia family, became a top notch newspaper and magazine journalist, and made her fictional debut with the well-received *Fly Away Home.* Her second novel is equally exciting and obviously drawn from the same deep well of personal experience transformed into art. Elizabeth Manganaro's mother supposedly committed suicide when Elizabeth was nine; her daughter never believed it, and 26 years later the recently widowed Elizabeth finds that her doubts were justified. She also finds that the truth can be very dangerous."

Ingram Books wrote a short review: "Determined to find the mother whom she is convinced is still alive, Elizabeth Manganaro travels to Los Angeles with her young daughter, unaware of the terrible price the reunion will carry."

1998 started out as an exceptionally good year for Susan. On Monday January 12, 1998, Susan was rewarded for her hard work on the A&E project when The Writers Guild of America, East and West announced its nominations for outstanding achievement in television and radio writing during the 1997 season. Susan's name was on the list. It marked the 50th Anniversary of the Writers Guild Awards and was celebrated in gala ceremonies on both coasts. Susan's nomination was for her cowriting work, along with Jim Milio and Melissa Jo Peltier, on *"Las Vegas: Gamble in the Desert."* Susan could not have been more happy or proud. She attended the dinner with her personal manager Nyle Brenner.

Kevin McPherson, a producer on the A&E project, worked closely with Susan for months. He said she worked tirelessly on the documentary and landed hard-to-get interviews because of her Las Vegas contacts. But working with her wasn't always easy, McPherson noted. "On the daily stuff, it was difficult," he said. "She was always worried. I felt sorry for her. It seemed her whole identity was derived from being the daughter of a mobster." The last time McPherson saw Susan was at the Writers Guild awards banquet.

Part 1 of the four-hour series first aired on the evening of Sunday, December 1, 1996. Part II aired the following night, on Monday, December 2, on cable's Arts & Entertainment channel.

Susan received glowing reviews for her work on the documentary. In one, headlined "The Voice of Reality," writer Melissa Jo Peltier glowingly wrote, for an article in the September 1999 issue of *Written By,* about Susan's role. Peltier, who worked beside Susan on the project, wrote:

> In writing the A&E special *Las Vegas: Gamble in the Desert* with my partner, Jim Milio, and our co-writer, Susan Berman, it was Susan's voice that determined the voice of the piece. Susan had grown up in Vegas and pondered the absurdity of its existence and significance for years. Although Susan, primarily a print journalist and novelist, had the most passion and the most clearly defined point of view about the subject, Jim and I contributed our craftsmanship in the genre. As her cowriters it was our job to help shape and define Susan's voice, while keeping

it intact. I believe it was the combination of our craft plus Susan's vision and passion that made this project worthy of the Writers Guild nomination for nonfiction in 1997. The experience helped me realize something simple: The documentary writer's voice comes as much from passion as it does from craft.

Likewise, in the November 28, 1997, issue of *Critic Pick*, a column titled "The Las Vegas Story" raved about the series. Writer A.D. Amorosi wrote in the *Philadelphia City Paper*'s November 28 to December 5, 1997, edition:

Frank, Dino, Sammy and... Debbie Reynolds? The A&E network's award-winning "Biography" series and author/mob daughter Susan Berman have collaborated on what can be considered the ultimate Las Vegas home companion. Their two-part product, *The Las Vegas Story*, is four hours' worth of garish gaudy fun, guns, gambling and politics and the insider's scoop on what it means to be in the ultimate city of lights. The daughter of Nevada mob honcho Davie Berman (partner to Las Vegas creator Bugsy Siegel), Berman takes an intimate look at Vegas history that's valuable, accurate and loads of twisted fun. Based on her books *Easy Street* and *Lady Las Vegas* (Penguin), the two-part series— *Gamble in the Desert* and *House of Cards*—features performers Alan King, Shecky Greene, Wayne Newton, casino owner Steve Wynn, journalist Nicholas Pileggi and a baker's dozen worth of local sheriffs, strippers, administrators and hangers-on. They mull over archival footage of Las Vegas from when it was a dusty prairie gambling stop for war veterans and Hollywood's elite up to its present-day cardboard family outlook. Along with two Rhino label CDs (Jackpot! and Soundtracks With a Twist) full of raucous, swinging Vegas types like Tom Jones, Vic Damone, Liberace, Anka and even Tony Scotti's "Come Live With Me" (from *Valley of the Dolls*), this glittering book, CD and TV package hits 21 every time.

Helping Susan Berman land interviews for the documentary were several people in Las Vegas. One was Deke Castleman, an editor for *Las Vegas Advisor*, a monthly newsletter, and Huntington Press, a Las Vegas publishing house. He explained how he came to help Susan with the documentary and accompanying book.

Susan Berman had a "long aversion" to Las Vegas, Deke told me. "It's my understanding," he said, "that she wanted nothing to do with the place for a couple of decades at least. But finally, in the mid-'90s, she decided to come to terms with her hometown—part nostalgia, part expiation, part paycheck.

"My details on the first deal are a bit fuzzy, but I think she pitched the idea of a long Las Vegas retrospective to a friend who owned a video production company. The friend then sold the package to A&E. And then, all of a sudden, Susan was face-to-face with the reality of doing four hours of TV on a city with which she had all kinds of history—mostly bad. And the fact was, she knew very little about Las Vegas post 1965 or so.

"So she went to Brentano's in L.A. and stood staring at the Las Vegas guidebook shelf for awhile. She decided to buy one book, pretty much at random, and picked *Compass Las Vegas*, which I wrote.

"Well, she got home, opened to page one, and saw that I'd dedicated the book to 'all the Jewish gamblers who helped build Las Vegas,' including Siegel and Greenbaum and Dalitz and her father, Davie Berman. I'd loved *Easy Street* when I read it years earlier. I was utterly moved by it; those could have been my own relatives. What can I say? It's a Jewish thing. And I was so inspired by *Easy Street* that I dedicated my book to these guys."

After eight editions of *Compass Las Vegas*, Deke Castleman had not changed the original dedication, "though the more I learn about Bugsy," he said, "the less I'm inclined to thank him. But what the fuck."

"Anyway," Deke continued, "Susan told me she nearly *plotzed* (Yiddish for fainted) when she saw the dedication, and she immediately got on the phone to try to track me down. She called Mike Tronnes, a very cool character from Minneapolis, who'd just come out with a book called *Literary Las Vegas*, a collection of excerpts of pieces on the town by creative writers, of whom Susan was one. I'd helped Mike a little with the book—even though he didn't excerpt me, the fucker—so he knew where to find me when Susan called asking."

What happened next, Deke said, was a pleasant surprise that launched his friendship with Susan.

"So there I am," he said, "sitting at the dinner table with my family in Las Vegas, when the phone rings. My wife answers and says, 'Yes, he is. Can I ask who's calling?' And then she turns to me and says, 'It's Susan Berman.' And I say, 'Susan Berman? *The* Susan Berman? *Easy Street* Susan Berman?' And I grab the phone and, well, you had to know her. She starts screaming.

"She'd get so excited that her voice would rise three octaves and fifty decibels, somewhere between hysterical and ecstatic, and she'd launch into a stream-of-consciousness narration.... I always felt I was coming in in the middle of a conversation with Susan. I never did find out the beginning or the end of what she was talking about. And the most amazing thing was, I wouldn't hear from her for three months, say, and when I'd pick up the phone and it was Susan, she'd just continue the conversation at the exact same place where we'd left off our conversation of three months ago.

"Anyway, this time she's squealing into the phone, 'Omigod! Omigod! I started crying! I mean, when I saw my father's name in your book! I'm so touched that someone remembered him. And I'm coming to Las Vegas and I'm doing this shoot, and we must meet! It was the only book I bought! Out of all the travel guides at Brentano's! It was fate! It was destiny! You're Jewish, of course! Do you have a big nose like the rest of us? We'll put you on camera! I'm staying at Alexis Park. What's it like? Is it the typical Las Vegas dive? And where's a good place to meet for dinner? You'll bring your wife—she sounds so sweet! And your kids! Do you have kids?'

"Obviously, after two minutes on the phone, I was totally smitten with Susan Berman.

"So she showed up and I met her at her suite at Alexis Park—a statuesque, handsome, intense, and fiercely intelligent woman. Half the time demure and subdued, the other half manic and neurotic. I hooked her up with a few people who wound up on camera—I never did. Little did she need my help, though. She had access like I'd never seen—her Las Vegas roots went very deep."

With Susan in Las Vegas was photographer Gerardo Somoza. He spent a day and a half taking promo photos for the documentary and accompanying book. "The photos I took were taken at the Flamingo [hotel], near the pool, in the casino, and around Las Vegas with her," he said. It was August 1996.

Gerardo said he got to know Susan by spending so many hours with her.

"We had lunch and dinner together," he said. "We talked a great deal, about her childhood and what she thought about the whole Mafia connection. She was definitely sweet, nice. She did whatever I wanted [her] to do, in terms of photos. She was a very nice person, but she was a little weird. You just had that feeling. It was just the way she was as a person.

"First of all, her look was completely odd. Her shoulders were down, droopy. She didn't have this great stature. She wore a T-shirt and vest with black pants. She changed into a red dress. She was tan. She was not completely sure of herself. She was definitely awkward with herself, insecure with her looks. But she was flirtatious with me.

"A couple of producers were with us. When we got to the hotel, the Flamingo, Susan told us, 'Oh, my God, the pool is almost the same.' She said there was a black curtain in front of the casino and she never crossed through it. She said the counting room scene in the movie *Casino* was incredibly familiar to her because it was exactly the same as the one in the Flamingo. I remember her talking about her dogs. She loved those little dogs. She said, 'They're my kids.'"

Somoza stayed at the MGM, other people involved with the documentary stayed at the Hard Rock Hotel, and Susan stayed at Alexis Park, a hotel and time-share parallel with the Strip, on Paradise Road. "We were in town for four or five days," Somoza noted.

While in Las Vegas doing her research and setting up interviews, Susan went to the Nevada State Museum, on Twin Lakes Drive in historic Lorenzi Park near downtown. As a child, she'd played at the park. Dave Millman, a historian and curator of the museum, met with Susan for three hours in the museum's library at a conference table. Later, she described him in *Lady Las Vegas* as "a little craggy-looking with a scruffy beard." His wife, Millman said, "didn't like the description very much."

In *Lady Las Vegas*, Susan wrote that as she left the state museum, David "asks me if I would consider leaving my family pictures to the museum in my will. I am touched. My family is history; my dad will be remembered."

Susan at age 5.

With mother Gladys at the
Flamingo pool.

Gladys and David Berman, Susan's parents,
at their wedding dinner.

The trio running the Flamingo and Riviera hotels: Willie Alderman,
David Berman, and Joe Rosenberg.

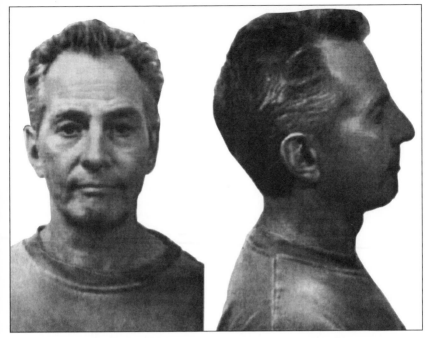

Robert Durst, a mug shot from the Galveston Police Department.

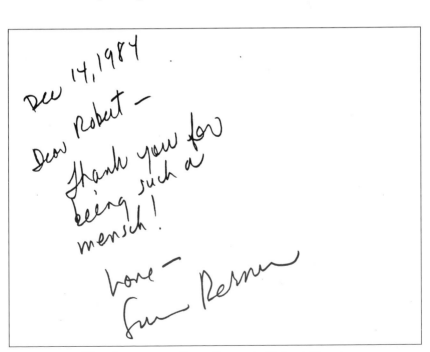

Thank-you note from Susan to Robert Durst.

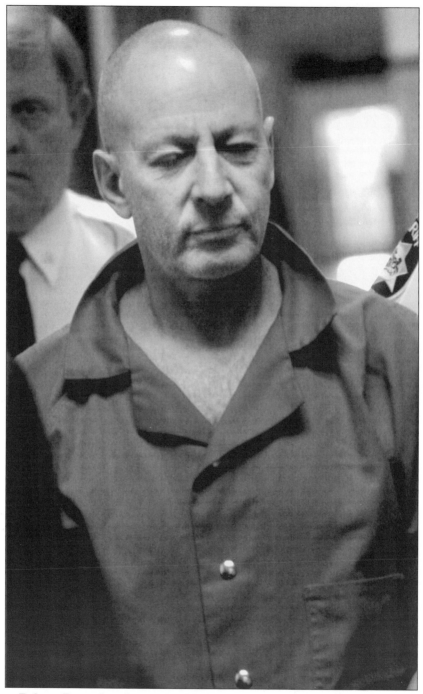

Robert Durst leaving a Northhampton County Courtroom after a hearing on Monday, December 3, 2001.

Susan's New York City apartment house at 30 Beekman Place.
(Photo by Cathy Scott)

The house at 1527 Benedict Canyon Drive
where Susan was murdered.
(Photo by Cathy Scott)

Susan with one of her wire haired terriers.
(Photo by Ruth Bartnoff)

The Home of Peace Mausoleum in East Los Angeles where Susan is
buried beside her parents and uncle.

Headstone for David Berman, "beloved husband, father, and brother."
(Photo by Cathy Scott)

Susan's headstone, "beloved daughter, friend, mother."
(Photo by Cathy Scott)

Susan at the Flamingo Hotel during the shooting of the A&E Las
Vegas documentary.
(Photo by Gerardo Somoza)

"She said she had photos of her family she'd give us for our archives," Millman said. "She never did."

He described her as "funny" and "a little nutty."

"She talked nonstop," Millman said. "She was very pleasant to talk to, and I enjoyed it, but she went a mile a minute. I could see how you could give up on her as a friend."

He said he'd looked forward to reading *Lady Las Vegas*. But after it came out, he said, "I was so disappointed. The book itself is not a good history book. Overall, it had a lot of mistakes. It repeats a lot of the myths. It appeared to be a moneymaker, thrown in to go with the A&E series. It had a lot of inaccuracies." Conversely, he said, the earlier *Easy Street* "was excellent and accurate." "And the A&E four-part series Susan cowrote and produced that went with the book was the best by far made about Las Vegas," Millman said. "That was certainly a high moment for Susan. It's the best ever done."

Susan also met with Rob Powers, public relations director for the Las Vegas Convention & Visitors Authority, Sheriff Jerry Keller, Nevada historian Hal Rothman, *Las Vegas Sun* publisher Barbara Greenspun, whose family Susan described as "politically active," Harrah's CEO Claudine Williams, Elaine Wynn, wife of casino mogul Steve Wynn, historian Guy Rocha, and a handful of old-time Las Vegans.

She also met with Deke Castleman, who became a close friend during the final four years of Susan's life.

Deke said Susan arranged for some heavy-hitter interviews used in the A&E documentary, getting those on camera who often don't want to go on, as well as helping a few others gain notoriety.

"She pretty much discovered [historian] Hal Rothman, who's a minor celebrity these days," Deke said. "She gave [publisher] Anthony Curtis some major exposure. She got the notoriously camera-shy [author] Michael Ventura. She even got Steve Wynn, who rarely does those kinds of interviews. When I asked her how she got him, she sort of dismissed the question with a wave of her hand and said, 'Oh, I just called his mother, Zelma.' She once regaled me with stories about Bugsy's two daughters, whom she knew."

Zelma Wynn was good friends with Susan's friend Ruthie Bartnof, who met the Wynns when the Bartnofs lived in Las Vegas.

Susan wrote about Deke Castleman with affection. Deke had found a phone book with Davie Berman's name listed. "Deke has gone to the incredible trouble of finding a Las Vegas phone book from 1956," Susan wrote in *Lady Las Vegas*. "So thin. So few of us then! 'Look, your dad was the only hotel owner who listed his phone number. There you are at 721 S. Sixth Street,' he says, kindly. I clutch the pages, thrown back for just a moment into the middle of my loving family, feeling the excitement of a floor show opening."

Deke remembered well when he gave Susan the listing.

"When I was writing the first edition of my Las Vegas guidebook in 1989," he said, "I went to UNLV Special Collections [office] and pored through every Las Vegas phone book; they have them all, from the very first one, 1923, I believe. I was looking, mostly, for the oldest restaurants in Las Vegas.

"Jewish gamblers I'd decided to dedicate the book to. I didn't expect to actually find any of them, of course. But there were the Bermans, in the '55 and '56 phone books, if I recall correctly, with their street address—the bungalow on Sixth Street—and phone number.

"I remembered from *Easy Street* Susan's description of how hard Davie tried to legitimize himself in Las Vegas; his name and address in the friggin' phone book were proof positive, as far as I was concerned.

"So one time when Susan was coming to town and I knew I was going to see her, I went back to Special Collections, requested the '50s phone books, found the Berman listing, and made a copy of the page. When I gave it to her, she was stunned—only time I ever saw her sincerely speechless.

"Her eyes welled up and I could tell she was remembering those carefree days when she was nine or 10 or 11, living in the house on Sixth Street, running around her daddy's casino—the Riviera, teasing Uncle Gus (Greenbaum, who's been described by people who knew him as one of the scariest men they'd ever met, and later had his throat slashed while he was sleeping in his house in Phoenix—they slashed his wife's throat too, for good measure) and Uncle Moe (Sedway, who did a lot of Bugsy's dirty work for him)... a time after which there were never any more carefree days.

"Of course, her reaction made me wonder whether I'd done the right thing by reminding her of her past. But she made me feel like that nickel Xerox was the most thoughtful and important gift anyone had ever given her. That's the way she was."

While Susan was in Las Vegas, Deke said, "she did take my family to dinner, at the Rio buffet. She instantly fell in love with my older son Adam, who was four at the time. Every time she called me after that, I'd pick up the phone, say 'Hello?' and I'd hear, 'How's my Adam?'

"So she shot the A&E show and went home, and then had to write the companion book. I spoke to her several times during that process, when she was totally stressed by the deadline, and helped her a little.

"After that, she'd call every so often to tell me about one cable TV deal or another she had brewing on Las Vegas. She told me that she was also working on a book proposal about the women who helped shape Las Vegas, and I gave her a few names of old-timers I knew.

"Toward the end she was trying to sell a series to Showtime, as I recall, sort of 'Friends' meets casino gambling, and she'd pick my brain about plot and character and inside stuff."

Indeed, among the current projects Susan proposed was a television documentary about Las

Vegas that focused on women, a pitch to ABC television for a movie based on her diaries, and a series once considered by Showtime called "Sin City."

Deke said the last time he spoke with her, Susan was "three octaves high again. It seems she was just about to close a big deal on the Las Vegas series and she promised me that I'd write one of the episodes."

Then, he continued, "A couple weeks later I heard that she'd taken a bullet through the back of her head."

Deke described Susan as "my soul sister. I loved her."

Shortly after her murder, Hal Rothman wrote a piece for *Las Vegas Magazine*. In it, he remembered the woman who had become his friend. Rothman, a history professor at University of Nevada-Las Vegas. An editor wrote, as an introduction to Rothman's article, "He remembered the woman who was shot to death at her Los Angeles home on Christmas Eve."

Susan's death, Rothman wrote, "robs Las Vegas of one of its best sources of oral history."

"The hyperkinetic Berman," he continued, "was the one scion of early Las Vegas to tell the story of growing up here, and she told it with honesty and clarity.

"Her 1981 memoir *Easy Street* offers the best look at Las Vegas in the 1940s and 1950s and from a child's point of view. Her later work, primarily A&E's two-part 1996 documentary *Las Vegas: Gamble in the Desert* and *House of Cards* and the accompanying book, *Lady Las Vegas: Inside Story*

Behind America's Neon Oasis, did what outside journalists never could. Susie Berman succeeded in simultaneously humanizing Las Vegas and keeping its edge. She laughed at the local obsession with trying to evade the city's mob past. She also embraced the city and its idiosyncrasies, showing how and why Las Vegas, at least when she knew it, really was different than the rest of America.

"I worked with Susie on the A&E special and the book that accompanied it. She created that project and carried it forward with her will, both for the city and as an extension of who she was. No one else alive could claim Las Vegas as an older sister, a competitor for affection, but with Susie it seemed natural. She loved this town the way it once was, when guys such as Gus Greenbaum and Willie Alderman were everywhere, and she came to understand the new Las Vegas with its corporate leadership and thousands of tourists walking in the heat.

"Before it was fashionable, Susie Berman held her head up and was proud to be from Las Vegas. Those of us who study the town will miss her."

In a telephone interview a year after Susan's death, Rothman said, "She had become a good friend. She was an all-around good person who wanted to get the story right. I feel a great loss."

Deke Castleman said, besides helping Susan with the A&E documentary, he also assisted her with her final project.

"Susan was working on a book," Castleman said. "It was on outstanding women in the gaming industry and the importance of women in the development of legalized gambling. She was still researching. I don't know that she had started interviewing. She said she had a publisher. She was so well set that way.

"We talked about so many people. She was looking for guidance. The first thing I told her to check was with the state because I know the very first gaming permit that was issued in 1932 was to a woman. I can't remember her name. I had sicked her on to Claudine Williams, Jeannie Hood, [and] Wilbur Clark's widow. We must have gone through a dozen or more [names]."

It was as if Susan had never left Las Vegas. Even though as she entered her teens she had moved to California and then to Oregon, her roots were firmly planted in the desert. Her life's work was invariably about the Las Vegas mob and her father's role in it. To her friends and colleagues, she seemed pleased at the acceptance of her work.

Susan was still a member of the Writers Guild of America, which has stringent rules for membership. It listed Susan's writing credits as an A&E "Movie of the Week," an A&E four-part series on Las Vegas (*Gamble in the Desert* and *House of Cards*), and as a writer in 1978 for "People TV" on eight episodes.

"She was doing signatory work," an employee at the Writers Guild office said. "She was doing work under a recognized production company. She needed to do that in order to be a member of the Guild."

Susan was always working on a "project," the

"next big deal," her friends said. The last weeks of her life were spent, along with a new agent, pitching projects to book editors and TV and movie directors. Her friends and family said she was at the peak of her career. Mostly positive things were in the works. As Deke put it, she was "three octaves high" again about the projects she had in the hopper.

Another former Las Vegan helping Susan with her final project was author Dick Odessky.

"She wanted to be a tough broad," Odessky said. "That was her wanna be. She came across to me as almost the grown up 'poor-little-rich girl.' She had been too shielded from life to appreciate what she was about. That was the impression I got. She was protected in every way. I found when I would talk to her, I would have to lead her along the path because some of it was beyond her knowledge, beyond her recognition."

Soon after Susan's murder became known publicly, one Web site, {www.organizedcrime. about.com}, received so many queries about her case that the site started a poll, asking readers, "Did mob figures order a hit on Susan Berman?" The Clark County Public Library in Las Vegas had a waiting list of three hundred people for her books, a list that, a library clerk said, had "grown threefold since her death." Also following Berman's murder, Amazon.com contacted several Las Vegas used book stores, including the most popular shop, downtown's Gambler's Book Club, seeking copies of Susan's books to fill their out-of-print orders. Berman's three novels and two memoirs sold for between $39 and $359 on both eBay and Amazon.

Her friend Danny Goldberg said he wished Susan had gotten as much attention in life as she was getting in death. He said she was in "a pretty good mood when I spoke with her not that long before she died, maybe a month or so. She was in good spirits. She was very optimistic about what was happening to her professionally."

"She was a great journalist," he continued. "Her magazine work for *New York* and others was great. The book *Easy Street* is an extremely emotionally powerful memoir. I think it will live on as one of the best to capture what it was like to grow up in a family of gangsters.

"On a personal note, I remember her sense of humor. She was one of the silliest, funniest people to talk to. She had a great, amusing, sardonic spin on things, a humorous perspective that she uniquely had on situations. She had a tremendous vulnerability and pain she walked around with, someone I felt never completely got over her childhood and the life she lived in Las Vegas. She wore her pain on her sleeve."

Then, Goldberg added, "With the articles written about her after her death, it does make me wish she would have gotten some of that attention while she was alive."

Susan's Last Days, Weeks, and Months

DETECTIVE BRAD ROBERTS of the LAPD's West Los Angeles Division homicide unit said Berman had paid her rent through March and was scheduled to move out in June 2001 after a long-running dispute with her landlady. Susan joked with her friends that she was going to end up homeless.

She hit up her friends for cash, about $1,500 at a time. But it was Bobby Durst who, over the span of their friendship, would loan her larger amounts. One check was for $50,000. Two checks, just months before Susan's death, were for $25,000 each. Bobby included a note that said, "This is a gift."

The final $25,000 check allowed Susan to settle up with her landlady. Baskin Schiffer would show up at Susan's house unannounced to argue about overdue rent, the dogs, and repairs; the standoff had escalated to a three-year eviction battle. Susan repeatedly told friends she was afraid of Dee and feared she would harm her dogs. In the days before she died, however, Susan paid her rent through March, and a lawyer had worked out an agreement for Susan to leave the property by June. She told friends she was relieved it was all finally over.

Also with the money from Bobby, Susan purchased a used SUV for $7,000. She finally got rid of the 20-year-old black convertible Chrysler she purchased years earlier when she moved from New York City to Los Angeles. Susan, unable to find Bobby because he had changed his telephone numbers, had sent Bobby a note via the Durst Organization asking to borrow $7,000 for a used vehicle. That's when he sent the first of two $25,000 checks.

"Susan was humiliated by her financial situation," her friend Stephen Silverman said, "but made jokes about it as best she could, calling herself homeless and the like, as if listeners were supposed to laugh. Mostly we would gasp."

Susan would often joke and end a telephone conversation with, "I'm going to get into the bathtub with my hair dryer now."

Susan was able to get freelance work, just not enough to pay all her expenses and, later, her back rent. Susan didn't look for full-time work. Instead, she went to friends. At one point, she even sold her mother's jewelry.

Ruthie Bartnof said she once suggested to Susan that she find permanent work. Susan was offended.

"It was the only time we had words," Ruthie said. "I told her, 'You know, I think it's time to find a way out of this.' She was left a great deal of money. I don't know what happened to it. For some reason, she just felt that it wasn't her heritage to work. She was really trying to grab what she'd lost when her parents died. There was so much money in the hotel business at that time. My instinct tells me that she was robbed."

Beginning in late November through the end of December 2000, Susan sent out Christmas and Hanukkah cards to friends. She was upbeat in her notes to them. In return, she received cards and gifts.

"We sent her a check for Hanukkah that year," Ruthie Bartnof said. "My son Kevin sent it this time. She was generous to people, very generous in her gifts. She gave me beautiful gifts. I have a Louis Vuitton handbag she gave me. When she had the money, she shared it with everybody. She had very lavish parties."

A few months before her murder, Susan was desperate to find an agent. She telephoned several friends, including Stephen Silverman, seeking help.

"We spoke a month or so before she died," Silverman said. "She left a message. She needed an agent. She was desperate to find an agent. Absolute desperation. She said she needed help and that she was on Prozac but it wasn't working." He said he thought to himself, "This is a woman in trouble."

Silverman did not return her phone call right

away. Instead, he said, he waited a week.

"I agonized over it," he said from his New York office. That's because, in his words, "Susan was a lot of work."

"She was a difficult person to be around," Silverman said. "She'd wear you ragged. She was always needy, needy, needy. Boy, could she drain you of energy. I wasn't up to it."

When he did speak with her, in November 2000, a month before her murder, he said she told him, "Oh, don't worry about it, I found an agent."

"The drama was over," Silverman recalled. "She said everything was going to be fine once the Showtime gig came through. She was always waiting for the big deal."

A neighbor said Susan was often away. "She wasn't home much," Marvin Karp said. "I'd occasionally see her in the backyard with her dogs. She kept very much to herself."

Susan wrote a holiday letter to her former dean Ed Bayley. He described it as "an upbeat letter."

"There were no ominous things in it," Bayley said. "She said she was going to get a ride up to Berkeley and come and see us in Carmel on the way, and that was right before Christmas." When asked whether it was Bobby Durst—who owned two houses in the Bay Area—who would be driving Susan to northern California, Bayley said, "She didn't say."

In October 2000, shortly before her death, Susan landed a lunch meeting with Mickey Freiberg, considered to be a high-powered and well-respected literary agent. A friend of a friend had arranged for Susan to meet with Mickey, he said.

"We had lunch at Cantor's [a kosher deli on Fairfax Avenue in Hollywood]," Mickey said. "She wasn't prepared. She didn't bring a proposal with her. She couldn't articulate what her project was. It was more like a free lunch. She seemed hungry. She ordered a big meal and ate it all."

Susan had managed to land an audience with Freiberg, a top agent who has represented screenwriters and authors in both Hollywood and New York for thirty years and sells projects to studios, production companies and publishing houses. That was Susan, according to her friends. She felt she was a great writer and shouldn't have to prove herself over and over again with the detail of a formal proposal in writing. Needless to say, Mickey Freiberg, at the time with the Artists Agency, did not sign Susan.

Susan was working on three projects. One had a working title of "Rich Girl Broke" and was based on her diaries. She had pitched it to ABC for a made-for-TV movie.

She also was profiling female high rollers in Las Vegas. She'd hoped to turn it into a miniseries called "Sin City." But Showtime Networks, which had shown an interest, even attaching *The Rat Pack* director Rob Cohen to it, turned it down.

The third project she was developing was "Diaries," a fictionalized account of the mob as told through the eyes of the women of both historical and current Las Vegas organized crime families.

Susan went back to her original *Easy Street* agent, Owen Laster with William Morris, to see whether he could place her projects. Laster, executive vice president of the William Morris Agency and also a well-connected agent, first met Susan in the late 1970s while she was finishing *Easy Street*.

"It was a terrific book," Laster told *Entertainment Weekly*, "and there was a tremendous amount of film interest in it. The book, I think, didn't do as well as we hoped, and the picture never got off the ground."

Laster said he had not heard from Susan for a year until she called him six weeks before she was murdered. "She said she'd been doing a lot of things for television and writing screenplays," he told *Entertainment Weekly*, "but she had an idea for two books and asked if I would look at the proposals."

He did.

"One of them was a continuation of her story," he said, that went beyond the *Easy Street* autobiography. "It just looked like a sad book," he said. "I didn't think I could encourage it." Susan's working title was "Rich Girl Broke." It focused on her life as a Mafia princess, growing up in the midst of the major players of the twentieth century La Cosa Nostra.

But the second proposal, Laster said, interested him. "It was about women in Las Vegas. She'd interview people and get their experiences," he said.

Laster asked Susan to send him a more detailed proposal. She promised to get back to him.

He never heard from her again.

"She was very outgoing, bright, she had a smiling, gay face," he said. "She was pretty. She was very excited about her book."

Susan also contacted Oscar Goodman, a mob-attorney-turned-mayor of Las Vegas. She contacted his office and mentioned a project, but didn't go into detail about what. "I've been waiting for a telephone call from the Los Angeles Police Department," Goodman told me. "I wrote a letter to Susan right before she died. It should either have been unopened in her mailbox or in her house. The LAPD never called me. I thought they'd be curious." He said Susan had contacted him and, in his letter to her, he was responding to her request for information about a project she was working on. "I didn't have any information that would be useful for her," he said, and that's what he told her in his letter.

Another Las Vegan Susan telephoned during the same time period was Dick Odessky, who, besides an author, was once a public relations director at the Flamingo Hotel.

"Susan had been seeking background information for her latest project, a special report on women in the gaming industry," Odessky said. "She didn't give any vibes of any problems. She was very happy with her work, and she seemed very pleased with the acceptance of her work."

Danny Goldberg said the same thing. He spoke with her often on the phone during the last months of her life. Goldberg last saw Susan on July 4th of the same year.

"I moved back to New York," he said, "but my

family and I would go to Malibu around the July 4th holiday, and I would see her on July 4th."

Nothing had changed in the last weeks of Susan's life. She was still cautious. Among her worries was an acute fear of heights. She refused to go above the ground level of a building without being accompanied by someone she trusted. She was afraid of being thrown out a window. And, her friends said, she was deathly afraid of riding in elevators.

She was cautious even with the telephone. "She was very circumspect about giving out her phone number and address," Deke Castleman said. "And she never picked up the phone when I called her. I always had to leave a message, then she'd call me back."

Susan also had just been to see a new psychic, something she had been doing for years. She told a couple of friends that the psychic said she was going to die a violent death. Her friends accepted it as just another drama Susan was experiencing.

Chapter 10
Circle of Friends

*I run on instinct, immediately like or dislike some-
one, make snap judgments, and never change my
mind. My loyalties to my friends and family run
deep and true, but I know I am not easy to know.*
—Susan Berman
from *Lady Las Vegas*

SUSAN BERMAN MADE a point of cultivating friendships with people who were successful in the entertainment, music, and literary arenas. It became an
art and a lifetime pursuit. Her networking paid off
in many ways. She was surrounded by people in the
business.

Susan's friends never knew precisely what to
make of Bobby Durst. All they knew was Susan
adored him. A photo was once snapped at a party of
Susan holding Bobby's face in both her hands. It was
typical of her doting, sisterly nature toward him.

To friends, Susan "generally gushed about him,"
Stephen Silverman said. "One always had the feeling that, for whatever reason—I somehow thought
it had to do with his vast wealth, though that could
have been my own personal bias—it would not be
wise to proffer any criticism about Bobby, as Susan

wouldn't stand for it. This was, it should be noted, a rather odd circumstance with her, given how she so adored ripping people to shreds behind their backs."

Throughout his friendship with Susan, and while living next door to her in New York, Silverman said, "Bobby Durst was around."

Kathie Durst, Gilberta Najamy said, understood her husband's friendship with Susan. "Kathie wasn't jealous of Susan," Gilberta said. "They were friends. They liked each other. But Susie was clearly Bobby's friend. She turned on Kathie after she disappeared, because Susie was protecting Bobby. And I was more of an antagonist with Susan than a friend, because I kept saying, 'Bobby killed Kathie.'"

Oftentimes, wherever Susan was, Bobby would show. Danny Goldberg also said that "Bobby was around."

"I met Bobby Durst briefly," he said, "close to 20 years ago, sometime in the '70s. Susan's friends were the closest thing she had to family, and Bobby was in her inner circle."

Nyle Brenner also commented about Bobby. "He's always been somebody in her life," Nyle told the *Los Angeles Times*. He noted that after police announced they were again looking closely at the Kathie Durst case, Susan mentioned she was "worried about Bobby [Durst]."

It wasn't only Bobby's intellect and wit Susan was drawn to; she was also attracted to his prestigious position in life. "Susan was a woman who had a lot of friends who were famous or near famous or formerly famous," her friend Linda Smith told *New York* magazine, "and she moved in circles that were very interesting for her."

While Susan was drawn to Bobby from the start, she was never attracted to him romantically. "Never," said Susan's close friend, Ruthie Bartnof. "They were like brother and sister." Bobby was simply a "guy friend." Her friends said, from the start of their relationship, it was always, "Bobby this and Bobby that." Susan referred to him as her "big brother," the older sibling she never had. She went to Bobby for advice about schoolwork. She was thrilled to learn that Bobby was Jewish. That was always a bonus for her, her friends said, to meet someone she liked, then find out he was Jewish like her.

While Susan had a loyal covey of friends, she was sometimes hard on people. She was famous for fallings-out with friends that could last for years. "If you pissed her off," Sareb Kaufman told *New York* magazine, "she was like, 'Fine, you're out of the Rolodex. *You* obviously have an issue.'"

Before her death, Susan had a tiff with Sareb's sister, Mella Kaufman. They never made up.

After her murder, Susan's friends were reluctant to talk about her to just anybody. They circled the wagons to protect Susan's name. Some had never met but knew of each other because Susan often mentioned each of them. In fact, Stephen M. Silverman said Susan talked so much about her friends that he was careful about what he said to her.

"Susan was a loose cannon," he said. "I know for

a fact that she once blurted out some gossip that was totally made up. I was there. I was careful what I told her after that. She would talk to ingratiate herself and claim to know information. Her mouth would open and the words would come spilling out. There wasn't time to think. I loved her but I'm not sure I liked her."

People who knew her well and those who barely knew her, described her behavior with the same word: "Manic." Susan often called on her friends from UC Berkeley. Elizabeth Mehren, who went on to become a national correspondent for the *Los Angeles Times*, said Susan sometimes called her out of the blue. Elizabeth was in the same class as Susan and stayed in touch until the mid-1980s.

"Her murder," Elizabeth said, "has troubled me all year."

Before her death, Susan was still working, even though she wasn't making enough money to pay her back rent and bills without hitting up friends for loans, which she attempted to pay back but rarely, if ever, could.

After Susan's death, her network of college friends spread the word that their former classmate had been brutally murdered.

"I called Richard Zoglin when I heard she died," Harvey Myman said. "I called Ed Bayley, who didn't know about it.

"If it was a suicide, it wouldn't have surprised me. I dealt enough with her to know that she just floated through life."

The last time Harvey saw Susan was around 1993 at a UC Berkeley reunion at his Studio City home, eight miles from Susan's Benedict Canyon home. He thought her behavior was strange.

"We had a journalism school reception at my house and she came to that with her cousin," Harvey said. "This woman once lived in New York but was afraid to drive across bridges. I gave her directions on the phone. She asked if there were any bridges. I told her, 'No.' It came up at the party. I'm up in the low hills. There are two ways to reach Sunswept Drive. On one there is a kind of embankment with a guardrail and trestles. I never thought of it as a bridge.

"When Susan came to my house she was kind of pissed at me that I hadn't warned her about the 'bridge.' I smiled and said I was sorry. It struck me as odd, since she once lived in New York on an island. I realized that she was genuinely upset that I had led her up a bridge. It was a mountain road. I would have sent her another route had I known. The charming part of Susan was eccentric. But that was pretty crazy."

New York writer Lisa DePaulo befriended a couple of Susan's girlfriends, including Hillary Johnson, a fellow writer. Lisa wrote two lengthy articles about Susan and quoted her friends. The articles were published, eleven months apart, in *New York* magazine and *Talk* magazine. Hillary, too, planned to write about Susan. She had talked to Lisa about it. She was hesitant to talk to me, she told me in a telephone conversation, because she planned to write her own book about Susan and wanted to save information about Susan for her own writing.

The *New York Observer* pointed out the sameness of DePaulo's two articles. Even more curious was the fact that Hillary Johnson had pitched a similar story to *Talk* magazine, only to have it accepted, then killed. The editors turned it away, they told her, because the idea was too much like Lisa DePaulo's *New York* magazine article. That didn't stop *Talk* magazine, however, from taking the piece instead from DePaulo and publishing it in its February issue (which, coincidentally was its last issue; the magazine folded), despite the fact that it too was similar to the first article.

The published *Talk* article, no doubt, came as a big surprise to Hillary. "I plan to write something about Susan, either an article or book, in the future," Hillary told me. Also surprised were editors at *New York* magazine, since they had DePaulo's story first; *Talk* magazine, instead, was given credit for breaking new information in the case even though it was regurgitated material.

Here's what the *Observer*'s Gabriel Snyder, in an April 21, 2002, "Off The Record" column, had to say about the second DePaulo article, which was picked up by two New York tabloids:

> Editors at *New York* magazine were surprised to open the *New York Post* and the *Daily News* on Jan. 2 and read about a *Talk* magazine story on Robert

Durst, the New York real-estate family scion charged with dismembering a man in Galveston, Tex., and also under investigation for the 1982 disappearance of his wife, Kathie, and the Christmas Eve 2000 murder of Susan Berman, a close friend.

Why the surprise at *New York*? Both newspaper stories were very similar, reporting that *Talk* had dug up new information suggesting that Berman had told her friends that Mr. Durst had confessed to her that he killed his wife. The lead to the *News* story was, "A former close friend of millionaire murder suspect Robert Durst said she was prepared to 'blow the top off things' just days before she was found shot to death, according to a newly published report." The paper then cited a conversation between Berman and actress Kim Lankford. The *Post* cited the conversation as a new report.

But the report wasn't new to *New York*. Lisa DePaulo, who wrote the Durst article for *Talk*, had previously written a story on Berman's death for *New York's* March 12, 2001 issue—and in her opening anecdote, she described the very same conversation between Berman and Ms. Lankford.

Was *Talk* touting Ms. DePaulo's warmed-over reporting as a scoop? I was a bit taken aback to see that both papers lead with something we reported a year ago, *New York* editor Caroline Miller told Off the Record. I don't know if it was pitched as new, or if there was some misunderstanding with the newspapers that this was new when it wasn't.

Ms. Miller did praise Ms. DePaulo's piece, saying it had broken new ground in the Durst saga. And the exchange between Berman and Ms. Lankford appeared deep in the *Talk* article, which had also dug up new anonymous quotes from Berman's friends saying that Mr. Durst had confessed to the murder of his wife.

Reached for comment, Ms. DePaulo said of the Lankford quotes, "It was newsworthy then and it's newsworthy now. The fact that it wasn't picked up in March was a bummer, but P.R. isn't my territory." She added, "It would have been remiss to leave it out."

Of course, relations between *Talk* and *New York* [magazine] remain touchy since Maer Roshan left *New York* last year to be *Talk*'s editorial director, taking several of his writers with him.

Mr. Roshan said that the article was simply provided to newspapers in full—apparently, both the *Post* and the *News* carefully screened it and came up with the same lead piece of information—and that *Talk* didn't have control over what they picked up. Lisa DePaulo's meticulously researched article is packed with new information and insights that she spent months reporting for us, he said. Her article for *Talk* is the most comprehensive study of the Durst case to date, and it speaks for itself.

Talk magazine ceased publication with that edition and closed its doors.

Linda Smith commented about the dynamics of Susan's friendships. "She definitely made friends for life," Smith said from her New Orleans home. "She didn't forget you. She had some very, very close-knit friends for life. It wasn't a circle of friends, although her closest friends eventually became friends with each other. Those friends got to be friends through Susan. It's a network."

About Susan's death, her former classmate Lou DeCosta said, "It's been 10 years since I saw her in Los Angeles at a Russian restaurant called Zorgi's. Her death was a huge shock.... Everybody was interested because of the mob connection and also because of the rumors about Susan. The word on her was that she was in debt up to her eyeballs. She was always trying to borrow money from people, was always dreaming bigger than what was likely to happen. It's sad. She really was a talent. She was a great and funny writer when she wanted to be."

Former UC Berkeley J-school Dean Ed Bayley said he and his wife weren't aware of Susan's financial difficulties. "She never asked us for money," he said. "We got a letter from her just before her death. She had just sold one of her TV scripts. She said this time it might get produced. She was very happy about that. She sold lots of scripts and they paid her up front for them but they didn't get produced."

Besides her old friends, Susan befriended several new people, mostly men, in the last years of her life. A handful worked on the A&E project with her and kept in touch afterward. One new friend was Nevada State Archivist Guy Rocha, in Carson City, who consulted for A&E. In 2002, 18 months after her death, Rocha was still grieving the loss of his friend. In *Easy Street*, Susan wrote that she chanted the *Kaddish* for her dead family. Rocha was touched by Susan's words. He, in turn, chanted for Susan.

"Susan used the first lines of *Kaddish* with the death of her father, mother, Uncle Chickie, and Aunt Lillian," Rocha said. "I was profoundly moved by this and her intent to carry on in the good name of her father.

"Early last year, and a few months after Susan's death, I visited Temple Emanu El in Reno to pay my respects to the congregation after the synagogue was fire-bombed by an Aryan hate group. During the course of the services, the Rabbi asked members of the congregation to chant *Kaddish* for those who had recently died. I turned to my dear friend Dennis Myers from KOLO TV 8 who had accompanied me to the temple and told him I would stand up and chant *Kaddish* for Susie. I cried while I chanted, remembering Chapter One of her book. In my own way, I did for Susie what she had done for her family. It was the least and the best I could do for this woman who had touched my life, if only briefly."

Before Guy worked with Susan on the A&E series, he said he didn't know who she was.

"I had a passing awareness of who her father was," he said, "but not who Susie Berman was. We worked on the project. I got a sense of who her father was. She mentioned it in passing. But I don't think, from that, anybody got a sense of the damaged person I got to know, I mean, emotionally damaged. Intellectually she was a sharp, bright lady trying to make her way."

Like many who knew Susan, Rocha was fascinated by his friend and her mysterious background. "I decided, in order to know Susie better, to read the book *Easy Street*," he said. "I read it and was moved by it. It was cathartic. Not only did I come to understand Vegas through her eyes—her father, his loss, and some insight into her career—but I came to know her other than professionally. When we had a reception in Los Angeles, in Beverly Hills at Planet Hollywood, it was powerful. [Entertainer] Rose Marie was there, and we had a chance to talk. Susie came in. She had a young man with her. I believe it was her son. We spoke. I told her I read *Easy Street*. I said, 'I understand.' She paused and looked at me, looked into my eyes. Then she said, 'You *do* understand.' I told her, 'You've suffered. You still suffer.' She said, 'I do the best I can. Sometimes life is hard.' Viscerally she knew I understood. She was damaged but she was a person who could pass for normal. I didn't always see a happy person."

Rocha felt what he called a "tremendous connection" with Susan. "I told her, 'I came from a damaged background too,'" he said. "We clearly established a common ground. I sensed a need on her part to have credentials. Part of that having credentials is who she associated with. I sensed deficiencies in self-esteem. She had all these pots boiling and things were cooking. At the time I was dealing with her, she was on an upswing. It was coming for her late in the game, but it was coming for her."

She talked "a mile a minute," he said. "She was really driven to talk. She didn't share everything, but when we engaged in a conversation it was hard to get a word in edgewise. She clearly had to *be* somebody. My speculation was that she didn't feel she was somebody. She overcompensated. I got to know her more intimately because of that visceral attraction of victim-to-victim. She was not self-aware. What I saw was someone who was so busy in her life that she didn't want to look at herself.

"She was damaged but not dysfunctional. That damage would play in certain ways that at times she would hurt others. She couldn't see it. She's one of so many people who suffer as kids and don't quite know what makes them tick. They have to prove something.

"We grew close in a very short time. It was a mutual respect. I was looking at conversion to Judaism. My life has moved in those circles, so here comes Susie Berman into my life. She intrigued me to no end, this career of hers that took her to San Francisco and New York.

"Then I pick up the paper, the *Reno Gazette Journal*, and I read on page 2 this happening in L.A., her murder. I said, 'Fuck. I can't believe it. She took a shot.' I still mourn her."

On December 18, 2000, a week before Susan Berman was murdered, Sareb Kaufman went out to dinner with her, just before he left for a holiday trip to Europe. "She was happy," he told a reporter. "She wasn't writing about anything controversial." And even then, he told a reporter, "she was interested only in the human aspects of these [Las Vegas] people. She wasn't hitting nerves."

While Susan may not have been hitting any nerves with her writing, she clearly struck a chord with someone crazy enough to do her in.

Jim Grady, a friend of Berman's and a former investigative reporter who covered organized crime for Jack Anderson's syndicated column, told the *Hollywood Reporter*, "She worked so hard to have a normal life and ended up having a real bizarre and abnormal death."

On the acknowledgment page in *Easy Street*, Susan thanked Bobby Durst, as she had in all her books, but offered a special thanks to Danny Goldberg, who helped sell the movie rights to her book, giving her the largest advance she would earn in her lifetime. The acknowledgment read, in part: "... and especially Danny Goldberg, who, when I considered stopping the search saying, 'It's just too sad. They all died,' told me, 'But you didn't. That's why you must go on.'"

Then, Susan wrote, as was typical for her at the beginning of her books, *L'chayim*, which, when translated from the Hebrew, means "To life."

The last four years of Susan's life, she met a new group of friends, all from Nevada. It included Deke Castleman, Hal Rothman, and Guy Rocha. She regularly phoned them. What was noteworthy is that she never mentioned Bobby Durst to them. In the 1970s and 1980s, Susan constantly spoke of Bobby to her friends, even though many had never met him.

But in the late 1990s, to her new-found male friends, she omitted his name from conversations. Was that because her relationship with Bobby had changed? It would appear so. He was drifting away from Susan, isolating himself. What Susan didn't know was that he was living several different lives, living as a a woman named "Diane Winn" in New Orleans, as a cross-dressing man with fake dark eyebrows and white mustache in Galveston, and, finally, as himself in Manhattan. Susan was totally unaware of Bobby's strange behavior. And that, her friends said, put her in danger. Even if Susan's friends had known about Bobby's increasing erratic and bizarre behavior, Susan was so defensive of him that her friends believe she may not have listened to them anyway.

On December 19, five days before her body was found, Susan began telling friends that she had information that would "blow the top off things." Everyone assumed she was referring to blowing the lid off of a mob case. Later, after her murder, they instead believed she had been talking about having damaging information in the decades' old Kathleen Durst missing persons case. Because Susan was a "drama queen," as some referred to her, friends did-n't push her for more information. They simply listened. The truth was, nearly everything was a drama with Susan. They couldn't tell when the theatrics were based in truth and when they were dramatically blown out of proportion. In retrospect, after Susan's murder, the saga appeared to be real.

Chapter 11

The Investigation

*I am never secure and live with a dread that apoca-
lyptic events could happen at any moment.... Death
and love seem linked forever in my fantasies, and
the* Kaddish *will ring always in my ears.*

—Susan Berman
from *Easy Street*

WEST LOS ANGELES Community Police Station
patrol officers responded to a radio call at approximately 12:30 p.m. on December 24, 2000, of "an open
door in the 1500 block of Benedict Canyon Drive" in
the Beverly Hills area of Los Angeles. The officers
entered the location and discovered a victim in the
bedroom of the residence. It was Susan Berman's
house and her remains.

She became the LAPD's Case No. 000825485 and
one of 548 homicides committed that year within
the LAPD's jurisdiction, up from 432 the year
before, for a 27-percent increase.

A year and a half after Susan Berman's body was
found, no arrests had been made.

Two detectives, Brad Roberts and Ronald
Phillips, partners in the detective unit at the West
Los Angeles Community Police Station at 1663

Butler Avenue, initially worked the Berman murder. They weren't in their office when the call from dispatch came in. It was a Sunday afternoon and a holiday. They were called at home, just after 12:30 p.m. They knew there was one female body in a house and that the woman had been shot to death. What they didn't immediately know was that Susan Berman was the daughter of a notorious casino operator and member of the Jewish mob, a man once wanted by both the FBI and Chicago Police. The detectives learned *some* history, however, when they walked into Susan's living room. Hanging prominently—and proudly—on a large wall in the front room was a police "Wanted" poster for Davie Berman, Susan's father. One of the names printed below the photo was "Alias: Dave the Jew." It was a Chicago Police mural of her father from when he had been wanted decades earlier.

There was no robbery, no ransacking of her house, no sign of a struggle, no noises coming from inside the house to alert neighbors or passersby of an argument. The lights were off in the house. And there were no eyewitness descriptions of a suspect. Susan had died like a character in one of her own books. Only, her friends said later, Susan wasn't there to solve it.

The irony of Susan's death was not lost on investigators nor on her friends, nor would it have been lost on her, had it been someone else. Susan Berman had gone from being a rich Mafia daughter to a respected journalist and screenwriter, only to end up a struggling, penniless writer, shot to death in the back of her head like a mob associate. Susan knew better than most the truth about Las Vegas history. She'd reconstructed her father's past in her writings, only to die like a character in a mystery novel. But she didn't have any recent or new information that would have caused gangsters to want her dead. And she hadn't been writing about anything that would irritate modern mobsters.

Susan was far removed from the mob and its activities. That Susan was shot once in her head had led to wide speculation early in the investigation that her work may have prompted her slaying. Police, months into the investigation, said they had not ruled out that scenario. Still, to them it looked like a copycat crime by someone trying to make it *seem* like a gangland killing. That Susan died living one step away from homelessness was another strong indication that she didn't have a close relationship with anyone tied to the mob. She would have been rich instead of poor, because the mob would have made sure her financial needs were met.

Detectives Roberts and Phillips began their investigation at the scene of the crime, starting in the bedroom where the body had been found.

Investigators confiscated the hard drive to Susan's personal computer, which was in her spare room, where her body was found. The computer reportedly was full of clues. Susan's Rolodex with more than 1,000 telephone numbers was also taken as evidence and pored over by detectives. No gun was found on the premises. But, at the scene, investigators did find a casing from a spent bullet used in a small-caliber weapon. It was the best evidence they had. If a gun were later found, ballistics tests could be done to match it with the bullet casing. A single round was fired, hitting the killer's target squarely on the back of the head. Susan obviously didn't see it coming, since there was no sign of a struggle. She didn't know what hit her.

A crime-scene team began dusting Susan's house for fingerprints, leaving black soot behind them.

The area was relatively quiet—besides the loose dogs and passing cars—when Susan's neighbor Marvin Karp, a physician, left Benedict Canyon for LAX airport to pick up his daughter. He'd left for the airport just before 12:30 PM, shortly after the neighbors on the other side of Susan's house told him they were going to call police about the barking dogs.

When Karp arrived home, two squad cars were blocking his driveway. He parked down the street and walked to his house. Sitting on the backseat inside a squad car were two of the dogs who had been roaming the neighborhood for more than 24 hours.

Karp asked a uniformed officer, "What's going on?"

"The lady in that house was murdered," the cop said, beckoning toward Susan's. "We're taking her dogs to the shelter."

"It was a *big* shock to me," Marvin later said.

Karp, shaken by the news, walked next door to

Susan's front yard. A detective in a business suit asked him a few questions. Marvin didn't recall whether it was Detective Roberts or Phillips.

"The most curious thing was that her dogs were in my yard," Marvin told the detective. "My first clue that something was wrong was the dogs running around outside. They were barking. But they were very friendly. I saw one of them make a beeline across the street. It was the little one that went across the street first. Then the big one went across. Then they ran back to the house, like they were going home."

Police have said they believe Susan had been dead for about two days. Susan's neighbors insisted she was killed late Friday night, more than a day and a half before her body was found.

Marvin Karp said, from his point of view, the murder happened on Friday night, December 22, "because the dogs were outside early Saturday morning. And they barked all night."

That was evidence enough for him, he said.

"I probably was home when it happened," Karp said. "I didn't hear anything, except the dogs. He [the gunman] must have used a silencer."

The other next-door neighbor, who didn't want to use her name, said she and her husband had gone to see a movie on Friday night. "We didn't hear or see anything," she said, then added, "Thank goodness." She told police she and her husband wanted to keep Susan's dog Lulu. The dog was Susan's favorite fox terrier.

Had the intruder pulled into Susan's driveway, either one or both of the neighbors would have seen him, plus he would have alerted Susan, because of the headlights and the sound of the motor. To get there undetected, he would have had to park down the street and walk to Susan's house. There was no sidewalk there; the area next to the street was covered in grass, thick foliage, and trees.

A year and a half after Susan's murder, Marvin Karp said the short conversations he'd had with police back in December 2000 were his only interviews. "I haven't seen police or anyone for a while. Nobody," he said.

Neither neighbor could fathom why such an inexplicable horror could happen there, right under their noses, unbeknownst to them.

"The police questioned us—a lot," said the neighbors, a husband and wife, on the other side of Susan.

They, too, were interviewed, but, like Marvin Karp, only on the day Susan's body was found. It was as if, Marvin said, police thought she'd been snuffed out in a mob hit and that the case wasn't worth pursuing further.

"They thought it was mob-related," he said.

Still, after police looked to Susan's underworld past for clues and found none, they moved on. Next, they looked at people Susan might have had disputes with. It was a short list.

One dispute was with her elderly landlady, Delia "Dee" Baskin Schiffer, who had been in a lengthy and nasty battle with Susan over back rent and her barking dogs. Schiffer had taken Susan to court to evict her. Susan had been evicted twice; twice she had beaten her landlady in court. But Susan had finally appeased Baskin Schiffer. She'd paid the thousands of dollars owed in back rent, plus paid through March, thanks to generous financial gifts from her longtime friend Bobby Durst. Schiffer agreed, in turn, to let Susan stay in the house six more months, until June 2001, to give her time to find another place to live. Schiffer seemed an unlikely suspect.

The second person police were interested in was Nyle Brenner, Susan's personal manager. She'd met him a few years earlier while walking her dogs on Sunset Boulevard. Friends who met Nyle remarked at how much he looked like Susan's ex-husband Mister Margulies. According to Susan's friends, Nyle and Susan had an argumentative relationship. But, in the last few years before her death, Brenner was the person Susan spent the most time with. While police were looking into the dynamics of the relationship, they stopped short of calling Brenner a suspect. After an article appeared in *New York* magazine all but saying Nyle was under investigation and was a suspect, LAPD's Lieutenant Clay Farrell said, in October 2001, that "Nyle Brenner was not considered a prime suspect. The only one calling him a suspect is *New York* magazine. They said that, not us."

While police officially said Brenner was not under investigation, they later searched his house and obtained Brenner's files. If nothing else, they said, he was being "scrutinized." Brenner has never been charged in connection with Susan's death.

Stephen M. Silverman, the old friend who regularly talked on the phone with Susan, said he'd never heard of Nyle Brenner. "Susan never even mentioned Nyle to me," he said.

But another friend, Ruthie Bartnof, said Susan talked about Nyle. "He was very helpful to her in many ways," Ruthie said. "They had an unusual relationship. I don't know how intimate they were. He would help her, go with her different places, escort her. I met him when I went to one of her book signings."

About two weeks after Susan's murder, a Reuters reporter interviewed Brenner and asked why he thought Susan was killed. "I'm entirely at a loss," Brenner answered. "I don't know that there was anything she was working on that had any relevance to the [current] Mafia."

He did say that before she was killed she was working on "several other projects" having to do with Las Vegas. "She had been talking to a lot of people in Las Vegas recently, people who'd had a past there."

Susan, he said, was sought out by people in the publishing and film industries for her expertise on Las Vegas. "She was such a gentle person," he noted. "It's a mystery. I just don't know what to think."

To friends, and sometimes reporters, Brenner's tone was much more harsh, criticizing Susan and telling people they had no idea what she'd put him through. Friends said he was openly bitter and verbal about her, saying he was "done with her."

There were no solid answers on why Susan died. And the trail was getting colder as time progressed. Police looked for motives. Just after Susan's murder, Sareb Kaufman told the *Los Angeles Times*, "It's shocking right now. She was a gentle woman who lived life with great caution. She loved a lot of people and she had no enemies, because if she didn't like you she would not let you get close. Nobody had the opportunity to develop a grudge."

To Reuters, Sareb said, "She would have done nothing intentionally to put herself in danger."

Somebody, however, developed enough animosity toward her to want her dead. Police from the start said the murder was not a random act of violence. Susan had been the intended, premeditated target.

Meanwhile, Berman's friends became alarmed when they couldn't reach her.

"I tried to call Susan," Ruthie Bartnof said. "Nobody answered. I kept calling and calling. I called my son. I said, 'Kevin, Susan isn't answering and her machine isn't picking up.' He said, 'Mom, there's something wrong.' She was having her eyes checked for glaucoma. I told him she probably had that done and wasn't home. He started making phone calls to her friends. The information he got was, 'Don't discuss anything on the phone. Don't talk about anything.' I didn't know what *not* to talk about. Later I said, 'How come it's not in the paper?

The whole thing was bizarre. They [police and her friends] assumed it was an underworld thing. Why would they [old mobsters] care? They're in their hundreds."

It wasn't in the newspapers because the police had not yet announced the death to members of the press. Rather, Susan was buried *before* the media were informed about her murder, the killing of a daughter of an infamous Las Vegas mobster. The omission was curious. The 187 call—denoting a homicide—went across the police scanner, routinely monitored by crime reporters and city desk editors. If reporters had heard it, they no doubt would have responded to the scene. But it was a holiday and newsrooms operate with skeleton crews on holidays. No one knew that Susan Berman, an author, journalist, screenwriter, playwrite, and mob daughter was dead. The public wouldn't know for another 11 days. Soon, Benedict Canyon Drive and nearby Clear View Drive would be crowded with detectives, uniformed officers, emergency personnel, curious neighbors, and other onlookers. Even when the media don't pick up on certain calls, the ensuing press releases inform them of crimes. In this case, the release wasn't issued for 10 days. Then, it didn't hit some newspapers for another couple of days.

Police denied anything other than the usual handling and processing of a murder investigation. Once police released details of Susan's murder, they were deluged with questions from reporters about the woman the media dubbed the "mob princess."

Publicly, Los Angeles Police Department spokesman Lieutenant Horace Frank told reporters that "investigators had no suspects and did not know the motive. Nothing appeared to be missing and there was no sign of forced entry and no signs of a struggle." Nearly every reporter asked about a mob connection.

Frank said, "At this point, we have no reason or evidence to support linking the murder to mob involvement. But at this stage, we would not discount anything. We are going to look at everything."

Then, Los Angeles Police Department spokesman Eduardo Funes said, "It's a terrible homicide. A motive hasn't been established yet."

Funes, however, hinted that police had some leads to follow up on. "They are looking into several clues, but nothing I can tell you about at this time," Funes told reporters.

Detectives worked the case from the third floor of Parker Center, the Los Angeles Police Department's headquarters. Named after former chief Bill Parker, it's located in the heart of Los Angeles's downtown command center at 150 North Los Angeles Street. The Robbery-Homicide Division is where the murders in the City of Angels are chronicled by investigators.

With the May 2001 high-profile arrest of actor Robert Blake in his wife Bonny Bakley's murder, the LAPD was looking to clean up its image and get down to the business once again of solving cases. With the heavily publicized Rampart corruption and ensuing scandal, the LAPD's image was tarnished. They were unsuccessful in solving the murder of rapper Notorious B.I.G. (A.K.A. Biggie Smalls) and received some negative ink with that case. With the Blake arrest, as one TV talk-show pundit put it, "The LAPD got him." They appeared to be turning around their image and concentrating on crime solving, especially high-profile murders.

LAPD Sergeant John Pasquariello explained the delay in solving Susan's killing: "It's a murder case," he said. "They take a while to investigate. There is no imminent arrest."

While detectives looked for evidence at the crime scene, Susan's body remained at her house until 6:30 PM, when it was taken to the Los Angeles County Morgue on Mission Street near downtown L.A. Susan Berman became county coroner Case No. 2000-08986.

Two days later, at 8:30 AM on December 26, Susan Selser, a medical examiner and doctor, performed the autopsy, said Craig Harvey, a spokesman for the Los Angeles County Coroner's office.

At the time of Susan's death, the coroner's office was conducting about 6,500 autopsies a year, 2,400 of which were handled as homicides. Susan's examination fell into that category; her death was listed by the medical examiner as "a homicide with a pending investigation." It was noted on the autopsy report that she had brown hair, brown eyes, was 66 inches tall (or 5-feet, 6-inches), and weighed 151 pounds.

She was not wearing jewelry; no watch, and no earrings. No scars, marks, or tattoos were indicated by the examiner. The only property brought in was her driver's license. Susan's body was positively identified by her driver's license, not by a friend or family member, Harvey said. Then the coroner turned over her license to the California Department of Motor Vehicles.

Three days later, on December 27, 2000, Susan Berman's body was released by the county morgue and taken by a van to the Hillside Memorial Park in Culver City. The body was formally released to mortuary officials there. Susan's funeral was scheduled for January 2, 2001. After the service her casket and body were taken by van to the Home of Peace Memorial Park in East Los Angeles, where her father, mother, and uncle are entombed. She was placed in a crypt next to them.

That same day, the murder investigation was moved from the West Los Angeles police station to the Robbery-Homicide Division at Parker Center in downtown L.A.

That's when the LAPD announced Susan's murder, on January 4, two days after she was buried and twelve days after her body was found.

Once the media got a hold of the story, published stories were fast and furious. In the days that followed the announcement of her death, headlines blasted the front pages of the *Los Angeles Times*, *Daily Variety*, *The San Francisco Chronicle*, *Las Vegas Review-Journal*, *New York* magazine, *New*

York Times, New York Post, and The Associated Press and Reuters wires. The headlines screamed: "Author shot dead at home," "Mob Writer Susan Berman Found Slain," "Mob Scribe Berman Slain in West L.A.," "Writer of Mob Book Found Dead," "Did Mob Author Die For Writing What She Knew?" "Mob Daughter Turned Author Found Slain," "Execution-style killing of one-time Mafia princess is a mystery," "Who Killed the Gangster's Daughter?"

Lieutenant Clay Farrell with LAPD's Robbery-Homicide bureau tried to explain the nearly two-week lapse in time between Susan's murder and the news release outlining her death.

"On the Berman case, West Los Angeles [detectives] investigated that for 10 days or so," Farrell explained. "Robbery-Homicide made the announcement to the media once the case came into our jurisdiction. The case was reassigned to us when it became apparent it would take longer [to solve]. There was an opinion that it would overwhelm the resources of West L.A."

Detectives Roberts and Phillips were officially off the case.

It was never made clear why the Robbery-Homicide division wasn't called into the case from the start, the day Susan's body was found at the scene of the crime. Did police assume it was a mob hit, and probably unsolvable, surmising there was no need to transfer the case to the elite Robbery-Homicide division? As a result, by the time the case did finally make its way to Robbery-Homicide, the trail was already cold.

Robbery-Homicide detectives Jerry Stevens and Paul Coulter (now retired and a private eye), caught the case.

At 5 PM Thursday, January 4, 2001, police released a belated statement to the media at large. They asked that news outlets hold off reporting Susan's murder until 5 PM, just in time for the evening news and after business hours. The press release read:

Media Relations Section
Office of the Chief of Police
150 North Los Angeles Street
Los Angeles, CA 90012
213-485-3586
213-847-1760 Fax

LOS ANGELES POLICE DEPARTMENT
PRESS RELEASE
Thursday, January 4, 2001

Writer Susan Berman Murdered
West Los Angeles - On December 24, 2000, at approximately 12:30 p.m., West Los Angeles patrol officers responded to a radio call of an "open door" on the 1500 block of Benedict Canyon. The officers entered the location and discovered the victim in a bedroom of the residence. The investigating detectives determined the suspect(s) shot the victim one time in the head. The motive for the murder is still unknown and no suspects have been identified.

The victim has been identified as Susan Berman, the daughter of David Berman. David

Berman and Ben "Bugsy" Seigel, [sic] were business partners who co-owned the Flamingo Hotel in Las Vegas until Siegel's death, leaving Berman sole ownership.

Susan Berman was a book author, producer, investigative journalist, and screenwriter. She wrote several books including *Easy Street* and *Lady Las Vegas*, and was a dual writer/producer at the San Francisco radio station KPIX. Berman also wrote as a journalist for *New York* magazine and the Francis Ford Coppola magazine. Her latest work was a screenplay for Showtime's hit sitcom "Sin City."

Please contact West Los Angeles Homicide Detective Ron Phillips at 310-575-8408 if you have any information that may assist in this investigation.

This press release was prepared by Officer Danielle Lee, Media Relations Section at 213-485-3586. For Release 5:00 pm PST

Following Susan's death, the *North Gate News*, a newsletter at UC Berkeley, published an article titled "Alumna Susan Berman Found Shot Dead in L.A." Then-journalism student Kamika Dunlap wrote, in part, "As a journalist, Susan Berman capitalized on her life as the daughter of a Las Vegas mobster.... When Berman, 55, was found shot dead on Christmas Eve in her rented West Los Angeles house, newspapers from Los Angeles to London writing about her life, raised questions, but no answers, about a possible mob killing. Police found no sign of robbery."

On January 27, 2001, investigators with LAPD's

Robbery-Homicide bureau put a security hold on the Berman case at the Los Angeles County Coroner's Office. The hold simply said it was done by "the investigating agency," coroner spokesman Craig Harvey said. It meant no forensic or evidentiary details and no death or crime-scene photos would be released.

The same day, "America's Most Wanted," a Fox TV crime show, posted a "Wanted" poster on its Web site, seeking tips in the murder of Susan Berman.

A few weeks into the investigation, Detective Brad Roberts told the *Los Angeles Times*, "We still got nothing on this one. No real leads."

Meanwhile, Susan's landlady fixed up the Benedict Canyon house Susan was murdered in. She replaced the windows, and had it painted inside and out. Even so, it was difficult finding a new renter.

"She had a helluva time renting it out, because she had to disclose the murder," Susan's neighbor Marvin Karp said. "It took her months. She finally found someone, an English fellow, to lease it."

By October 2001, 10 months after Susan's death, Homicide-Robbery Detective Stevens, now assigned to the case, told me, "We haven't made an arrest and won't be making one soon. But we're not finished with this investigation." At the time, he said Nyle Brenner, Susan's manager, was not considered a prime suspect. Was he *any* kind of suspect? "No comment," the officer said.

The trail was getting cold quickly.

Chapter 12
The Mob-Related Theory

No one got killed that wasn't supposed to be.
—Debbie Reynolds
The Real Las Vegas

FIVE DAYS BEFORE she was murdered, Susan Berman told a friend she had "information that was going to blow the lid off things."

"What do you mean?" her close friend, actress Kim Lankford, in a retelling to *New York* magazine, said.

"Well, I don't have it myself," Susan answered, "but I know how to get it."

The next question could have been, "Get what?" But no one ever found out. And, after her death, they could only speculate. Lankford warned Susan to "be careful."

Susan's life, her friends said, revolved around one drama after another breathless drama. So when Susan would talk like that, they didn't take her seriously, like the boy who cried "Wolf" one too many times. Susan's friends assumed she was referring to a mob case. In retrospect, after her death, friends said they wished they'd paid more attention.

The mob-hit theory in the Susan Berman case turned out to be nothing more than interesting. Susan's friends were vocal to police and the media about their doubts in the theory from the start.

Detective Roberts told a pool of reporters, "We are looking at a few different things, even the Mafia, the mob thing, but it seems so remote and far removed. She was a mob daughter, and that was how she was making a living. But in talking to her family and friends, she had no connections now whatsoever."

Mob hit or otherwise, Susan's murder looked orchestrated.

"Normal people don't kill each other that way," Jonas McCord, a Hollywood director and onetime writing partner of Susan's, told *Entertainment Weekly*. "They go crazy. They shoot five or six times. They use really big [caliber] guns. This was, I believe, a professional killing."

Dick Odessky, a journalist who worked in public relations at the Flamingo beginning in 1961 and knew Davie Berman, doubted Susan's murder was a mob hit.

"When this all broke," he told me, "everybody was trying to lay it on the mob. Forget that. First of all, just in talking to her, she wasn't really afraid of anything, and, second, if it had been the boys coming to her for something that her father did or didn't do, the people who would have wanted to do that are either dead or so close to dead that they wouldn't have been able to hold a gun. It almost had to have been someone she knew. It doesn't make any sense."

Odessky, who authored the book *Fly on the Wall*, which included Mafia life in Las Vegas, talked to Susan on the phone for between one and two hours about two days before her body was found.

"As far as the mob is concerned," Odessky said, "the mob as we knew it is gone."

Sareb Kaufman, Susan's surrogate son, agreed. "There's a theory going around that the mob did it," Sareb told *New York* magazine, "but I don't think so. I don't think they would have anything to do with this."

Susan often talked about the mob to friends. "But she was very careful about what she wrote," her friend Ruthie Bartnof said.

Several weeks into the Berman investigation, police said the mob theory was, unofficially, ruled out.

And the Chicago Mafia-style contract hit was ruled out as well. Chicago-mobster murders historically have been done using a 22-caliber weapon fired at point-blank range to the back of the head. Susan was killed at close range—but not point-blank with a barrel against her head—from a 9-millimeter pistol. Former mob attorney Oscar Goodman said a .22 "is used in Chicago-style" killings.

John L. Smith, a columnist for the *Las Vegas Review-Journal* and an author, on January 7, 2001, had this to say about the manner in which Susan was murdered:

"As Susie told it, she was the Las Vegas version of *Little Miss Marker* who meandered through her father's glamorous, gaudy world as a princess in ponytails. Until his death in 1957, Dave Berman was a big man in Las Vegas at a time when the city was operated by characters straight out of *Guys and Dolls*."

Smith wrote that "Susie Berman crafted a successful career as an author and screenwriter out of that image. In her book *Easy Street*, she painted a neon-hued memoir of her young life with her family, including her uncle, Chickie Berman, that betrayed her wisecracking exterior and revealed Susie as a not-so-tough girl who still longed for attention from her daddy.

"When I heard she had been murdered on Christmas Eve in her Benedict Canyon home in West Los Angeles, I anticipated someone would attempt to link her fascination with the mob with her demise.... That she was shot with a single bullet in the back of the head only added to the mystery of a potential mob hit on the former Mafia princess.

"But think about it. A mob hit on Christmas Eve? Not even Hollywood writes such awful stuff.

"Even cat burglars take off Christmas Eve.

"Truth is, Berman didn't know two things about the mob and had very little knowledge of her father's world. That's what made her memoir so touching.

"Although she was a successful writer for *New York* magazine and the *San Francisco Examiner*, the kind of reporting that generates death threats wasn't her thing. As one person who knew her well recalls, she probably had never called an FBI agent or covered a mob trial.

"When LAPD detectives make an arrest, most likely it will be someone Berman knew and not some mysterious La Cosa Nostra button man in a fedora and overcoat. The fact that the case is being handled by West L.A. detectives and not LAPD Robbery/Homicide, which investigates mob-linked murders, is a giveaway. California police sources confirm their investigation is leading away from something as nefarious as an organized crime killing."

And in a later column, Smith wrote that her case was a murder mystery that Susan Berman would have loved to write about.

Casino author Nicholas Pileggi worked with Berman for a couple of years at *New York* magazine. The year before she died, she called him to discuss projects she was working on. "It's so befuddling," Pileggi told Smith. "It just doesn't make any sense at all, and it clearly doesn't make any sense in association with organized crime. She wasn't an investigative reporter. Her interest was in the social mores of that world and what it was like being a girl raised by the cast of *Guys and Dolls*. That's the way she looked at her father."

Pileggi continued, "She was very smart, very

deft, and a very good writer.... And she was a little girl right out of that Damon Runyon world."

Susan's cousin, Deni Marcus, also was skeptical about the mob theory, telling a reporter with *The Good Gambling Guide* in the UK that "whoever committed this act of violence, maybe they did it this way to make it look suspicious, to keep people guessing at some silly notion."

Indeed, that would be what it came down to.

Detectives attended Susan's funeral 11 days after her body was found. "We had a presence there," Lieutenant Clay Farrell told me.

It's common practice for police to go to funerals of murder victims to see who attends—and who does not. LAPD detectives assigned to investigate the Berman murder stood on the sidewalk in front of the memorial park, closely observing mourners. Nearby, an officer, standing behind some trees and bushes so he wouldn't be noticed, snapped photos. What was striking about Susan's funeral was that Bobby Durst, one of Susan's dearest friends, was conspicuously absent. It was noted by her friends, but, more importantly, by detectives.

Former Nevada Governor Bob Miller, who knew Susan as a child, had this to say about the LAPD looking toward the mob for answers: "Her level of information about the mob wasn't to the point where someone would want to kill her. The initial reports about it being a mob hit didn't make sense."

Miller said he learned about Susan's murder from her manager Nyle Brenner.

"I first heard about her murder when her business manager called me," Miller said from his Las Vegas law office. "He told me about the circumstances surrounding her death. I told him, 'God, that sounds bizarre.' Her son [Sareb Kaufman] called me about the services. I spoke to him a couple of times. I couldn't go to her funeral."

Sareb asked nine people to speak about Susan at the Writers Guild memorial service. Friends later said the anecdotes were touching and funny. The room was full of some of Susan's favorite people: mystery writers, screenwriters, and journalists, people who knew, like Susan, how to turn a sentence.

Speculation at the memorial service also arose about Nyle Brenner and what some considered to be his odd behavior. After notifying Sareb Kaufman, who was on a holiday trip in the Netherlands, of Susan's death, Brenner picked up Sareb at the Los Angeles International Airport. Nyle reportedly bad-mouthed Susan to Sareb. He continued to do it, friends said, the night of the memorial. That's when several friends either had a conversation with Nyle or overheard bits and pieces of his unsettling conversations with others. "At least I won't have someone calling me three times a day," Nyle told one attendee. "She sucked me dry," he reportedly told another.

Nyle also told Susan's friends that he had peeked through her windows after police left the scene and saw black soot on the floor. To others, he said he went inside but didn't see anything out of the ordinary, completely missing the dried blood and lock of hair on the spare-room floor where her body once lay.

When I reached Nyle Brenner by telephone at his office, he at first said he could loan me photos of Susan. Then, he said, "Everybody says they're going to write something and use photos. No one ever does. Forget it. The Associated Press said they were going to and they didn't," and he hung up. In a later telephone conversation, Brenner told me, "Anything about Susan doesn't interest me. I'm way past that. I just can't take it anymore. She wasn't the easiest person to get along with. I'm done with her. I have work to do and I can't be bothered. I have a business to run. I don't want to talk about Susan." He hung up the phone without saying goodbye. His business was managing and representing mostly B-grade actors, according to information listed about him on the Internet.

Investigators found no reason to pursue Nyle Brenner as a suspect and found nothing substantial in their investigation of the "mob-hit theory."

Chapter 13

The Missing
Persons Case

If anything ever happens to me,
don't let Bobby get away with it.
—Kathleen Durst,
to a friend

NINETEEN YEARS BEFORE Susan Berman was
killed, Kathie Durst was a 29-year-old medical student who had been married to Robert Durst for ten
years.

Four friends—Kathy Traystman, Eleanor
Schwank, Gilberta Najamy, and Dr. Marion
Wellington—said Kathie Durst had given them a
directive that if anything should happen to her,
"Bobby did it." That was just after Christmas in
1981. The night Kathie Durst disappeared she was
at Gilberta Najamy's Hampton, Connecticut, house
when Gilberta said Kathie received the last of a bar-
rage of phone calls from Bobby demanding that his
wife return home.

The last conversation Gilberta had with Kathie
was when she told her she was afraid of what her
husband might do to her.

That was January 31, 1982. Kathie Durst has not been seen or heard from since.

In 1998, New York State Police Investigator Joe Becerra unknowingly embarked on the case of a lifetime. The arrest of a flasher by the name of Timothy Martin started it all. Martin was looking to make a deal.

"He wanted to have a sit down with me and said he had information regarding this woman Kathie Durst from Lake Truesdale," Becerra told reporters.

At the time, Becerra had never heard of Kathleen Durst. When she disappeared in 1982, Becerra was still in high school.

He pulled the police file and educated himself by reading as much about the case as he could. He learned that Kathie Durst vanished in January 1982, apparently from the lakeside cottage in South Salem she shared with her husband.

Timothy Martin, looking to trade favors with authorities, told state police he knew what happened to Kathie Durst. "The information that he provided did not pan out, but it did get us to look into this case some more," Becerra said.

Following Detective Becerra's reopening of the Kathie Durst case 18 years after her husband first reported her missing, investigators dragged the bottom of nearby Lake Truesdale. A body, however, was not located.

"The lake, the house, and the property was [sic] all searched at various times, but I can't go into particulars at this point on what was and was not found," Becerra told Westchester News 12.

Westchester District Attorney Jeanine Pirro, who spearheaded the once-dormant investigation, said with confidence that sooner or later "we're going to find out what happened to Kathleen Durst."

Still, officials were slowed down when Bobby Durst refused to cooperate or even talk to investigators.

"Robert Durst has the right to remain silent and he has refused to cooperate with us," Pirro told News 12.

Gilberta Najamy has been vocal about Kathie Durst's disappearance since 1982. But she doesn't credit herself for the reopening of the investigation.

"The only hero in this case is Joe Becerra," Gilberta said. For nearly 20 years, she said she tried to find answers. "Detective Becerra has been at the helm, continuing the investigation."

Najamy was adamant that New York City and state police in the 1980s allowed Bobby Durst to get away with murdering his wife because of who he was: the son of one of the most powerful real estate developers in Manhattan, a man with clout. Durst initially had been investigated as a suspect in his wife's disappearance but was never charged or formally named a suspect.

"When I said that Bobby'd murdered Kathie, no one believed me," she said. "Now they do."

Initially, Kathie's disappearance gripped New York City for months but eventually faded from the headlines. Now, nearly twenty years after Kathie's disappearance, the pieces of the cold missing persons case started coming together, like a puzzle. Detectives dragged Lake Truesdale by the stone cottage in northern Westchester, combing the lake bottom for a body. The lake borders the Dursts' former country summer home. Investigators also searched the house. They removed a piece of a wall from the cottage.

After Kathie's disappearance Bobby went silent, with Susan Berman serving as his mouthpiece to the media and the police. Kathleen Durst had vanished days after she told her husband she wanted a divorce. Police strongly suspected Kathie was murdered and were following up on new leads, including Susan Berman. Then Susan was killed.

Upon hearing of Susan Berman's death, state police expressed extreme disappointment. Susan was not the only person authorities were looking to interview; they were reinterviewing and questioning everyone connected to the case. But Susan was considered a key person who investigators were looking forward to reinterviewing, hoping she'd shed light on the case.

Westchester County District Attorney Jeanine Pirro had this to say about Susan's death: "Miss Berman was a friend and spokesperson for the Durst family. When our office reopened the missing persons case about two years ago, the entire case was reviewed and there were reinterviews in the case. Susan Berman was one of the individuals that this office was very interested in. Definitely, she was a person we were interested in speaking to."

Chapter 14

Morris "Jack" Black

IT WAS SUNDAY, September 30, 2001, when a 13-year-old boy, looking for minnows while his step-father fished in a shallow area of Galveston Bay off Channel View Drive, made the grisly discovery of a dead body. He noticed it floating and bobbing in the water. At first he thought it was a pig. It turned out to be a headless, armless, and legless human torso.

Police later found the arms and legs, in separate black plastic trash bags, in the water 80 feet from the torso. The body was identified as that of Morris "Jack" Black. Black had lived across the hall from Bobby Durst. Police didn't find the head.

The dismembered body of 71-year-old Morris Black was pulled out of Galveston Bay the same day. Six months later, on Wednesday, March 27, 2002, Bobby Durst confessed to killing Black, but said, through his attorney in court, that it was an "accident" and was done in self-defense. Attorney Dick DeGuerin declined to elaborate after the hearing about why Bobby chopped up Morris's remains, saying he was under Judge Susan Criss's gag order.

To the court, DeGuerin said his client's admission would eliminate the need for DNA evidence. The attorney requested a three-month trial delay because he had not received the autopsy report on Black. The request was granted. The trial of Robert Durst for the murder of Morris Black, originally scheduled for June 2002, was reset for September 9, 2002, then postponed until February 2003.

Hang around the port city of Galveston, a wind-blown town, long enough, and you learn about the ebb of tides and currents, and exactly when and where *to* and *not* to toss a body into the water. That's what Bobbi Bacha, a private eye who grew up in the area, said.

"The water's deep," Bacha said, "but the current washes everything to shore, including bodies."

A newspaper asked for Bacha's help in finding Black's relatives. After the search, in which she successfully located Black's estranged family, Bacha continued working on the case, she said, for herself.

Bacha and a dive team went on two searches hoping to find Morris's missing head. They didn't, but they found women's clothing and wigs. They also found makeup, including unused lipstick still in packages, eyeliner, and mascara. After Bacha was quoted by several newspapers, Judge Susan Criss, who coincidentally happens to be Bacha's distant cousin, issued a gag order in the case.

"She [the judge] needs to recuse herself," Bacha said, "because we have the same great-grandfather. We're second or third cousins. We're not close, but we're blood cousins." The judge, however, did not remove herself from the case.

Reached for a second time at her Houston office, Bacha said, "My cousin is mad at me. She doesn't want me talking about the case. There's a gag order on me."

But before the gag order, which was placed on everyone connected to the case, Bacha said police were led to Durst's building after they found a copy of the *Galveston County Daily News* with an address label on it in one of the garbage bags containing Morris's limbs, leading them straight to Bobby Durst's run-down apartment complex. Blood in the hallway, leading to Durst's apartment, prompted a search warrant. Police searched Bobby's apartment and found traces of blood throughout the apartment as well as a bloody knife and boots. They obtained an arrest warrant to thoroughly search the premises. Bobby Durst, who was still in the area, was arrested October 9, 2001, while in his car. Located in his car, among other things, was a 9-millimeter handgun.

Bobbi Bacha said Black's missing head was crucial evidence in the murder case against Robert Durst. It would show the cause of death. Galveston

Police also were anxious to find the head. Bacha's search was done in an area where Black's limbs and torso were found. Six private investigators waded through waist-deep water while two divers searched farther offshore. A Galveston police officer was on hand. The divers came up empty.

Attorney DeGuerin said neither he nor his client knew the whereabouts of Black's head.

Even after Bacha's work for both the Galveston paper and the Black family was finished, she continued digging into the backgrounds of people connected to Bobby Durst.

"I'm not doing research for anyone," she said. "I like to finish what I start. I looked for Morris Black's head, did what I could, and, in the process, started looking at more things."

The question that begged to be answered was why Durst killed Morris Black, then chopped up his body.

The autopsy of Black has suggested that Bobby Durst had severely beaten him before he killed him. The report, released by a judge, also showed that Black fought back. Black's body had multiple bruises in an area 6 by 2-1/2 inches in the center of the chest. A triangle of bruises were on the right side of his chest. There were bruises on his shoulders, upper, mid, and lower back, left leg, and elbows. And a bone in his upper right arm was broken in four places. The most shocking aspect of the murder was that Black was beheaded and dismembered. The autopsy report said cuts in the muscle were sharp and "without significant fragmentation," meaning Durst knew what he was doing when he carved up Black's body.

The autopsy also revealed a series of parallel cuts on Black's right and left index fingers, suggesting Durst tried to cut them off, which would have made identification of the waterlogged and decomposing body difficult and near impossible.

For more than 20 days, Morris's dismembered remains were at the Galveston County Medical Examiner's Office before members of his family knew he was dead. Then Bobbi Bacha, an investigator for Blue Moon Investigations in Webster, Texas, was asked by a Galveston newspaper reporter to help locate Morris's family. The police, she said, weren't looking for them, so, as a favor, Bacha started to search. She found Morris's sister Gladys Black first, she said, through Morris's brother Harry's ex-wife Trudy, and then the others. Another brother, Melvin Black, she learned, died four years earlier in an insane asylum in Norfolk County, Massachusetts.

Bacha said Morris was a loner who could be cantankerous. He drifted from state to state, living in sparse surroundings without a telephone, losing touch with his family

At the time of Durst's arrest, Galveston police thought they'd arrested a destitute transient. Standard bail was set. There was a $250,000 bond for the murder charge and a $50,000 bond for a possession of marijuana offense. Durst posted the bonds, then took off. It was only after he put up bail that Galveston police learned that Westchester County, New York, law-enforcement officials had reopened an investigation into the disappearance of Durst's wife and that he was a wanted man. A nationwide manhunt was put into place.

"We had no idea who he was," said Galveston Police Lieutenant Michael Putnal. "Here was a man living in a $300-a-month apartment, who didn't have a telephone and who wouldn't have looked out of place standing on the corner outside the Salvation Army."

Assistant District Attorney Kurt Sistrunk echoed Putnal's statement, saying, "We were not aware of any criminal record. All this New York stuff came to our attention *after* we made our [bail] recommendation. He said $20,000 was the usual bond for first-degree murder. We went out of our way to set a very high bond."

Later, Putnal told reporters, "Clearly, he was acting like a fugitive long before Morris Black was killed. He seemed like a strange character to begin with. He was acting like he was running from the police long before Galveston had reason to take an interest in him. To me, that just adds to the level of suspicion in his involvement in the other crimes."

Galveston PD's "Wanted" poster on Durst stated that police believed him to be "armed and dangerous" and that "he may be dressed as a woman to avoid detection." In addition to the Black murder charge, Durst had other legal problems: On October 29, 2001, Morris Black's sister filed a notice of intent to sue Durst in civil court over her brother's killing.

Jim McCormack, Kathie's brother, was surprised Durst was allowed to go free in Galveston.

"I'm flabbergasted," McCormack told the *New York Post* when he learned Durst was free on bail. "It's an amazing circumstance. Here you have a man who is arrested and charged with an obviously heinous crime—based on being tied to the crime by physical evidence and a tipster—and he's allowed to walk free on bail. How could you allow this man to get back in society?"

Morris Black never married and had no children. Private investigator Bacha said Morris was friendly with Galveston resident Trudy Black, who told Bacha that Black had several bank accounts and asked her to collect the money if anything should happen to him.

While Morris had no visible means of support, police located several of Morris's bank accounts in South Dakota, one of which contained more than $137,000. Police speculated that Bobby Durst had been giving Morris money. Morris was a merchant seaman decades earlier and, for a brief period, a watch repairman. He also worked in building maintenance. But he never made that kind of money.

In January 2001, Morris Black rented an apartment in a four-unit building in a low-rent section of Galveston. Bobby Durst, estranged from his wealthy family for a decade, moved in in early summer, across the hall from Morris. Durst paid $300 a month for the sparse unit while simultaneously leasing a luxury condominium in Dallas and owning two homes in San Francisco, California, one in Colorado, and two in New York City's expensive Manhattan borough. Police didn't know why Durst moved into the four-plex nor had they uncovered whether Durst and Morris had known each other before Durst moved to Texas.

Galveston Police recovered a 9-millimeter handgun from Durst's car. Los Angeles Police traveled to Galveston after Durst's arrest. Ballistic tests were done on the gun by Galveston police, and the results were given to Los Angeles police, LAPD Lieutenant Clay Farrell said. The results, however, were not made public. Galveston police also found another handgun, a 22-caliber, in a trash can behind the K Street four-plex that Durst and Black lived in.

Durst was first arrested October 9, 2001 while driving his Honda CRV and was found to be in possession of marijuana and the handgun. He was released the next day after his second wife, New York real estate broker Debrah Lee Charatan, 44 at the time of Bobby's arrest, posted the $300,000 in bonds. Bobby was free.

Police later discovered that the man living in the cheap Galveston apartment was, in fact, the Robert Durst of the billion dollar Durst Organization, a real estate empire, and was from New York, not the poor, simple man police thought he was. Authorities immediately froze $1.8 million from one of Durst's accounts and suspected he might have had at his disposal other accounts with similarly large amounts of cash.

The following Galveston Police press advisory was released to the media after Bobby Durst made bail and skipped town:

> On September 30, 2001, a 13-year-old boy discovered a human torso floating in the water of Galveston Bay off of Channel View Drive. The body's legs, arms and head were deliberately severed. The arms and legs were recovered in the water approximately 80 feet from the torso. The arms and legs were in separate plastic trash bags.
>
> The follow-up investigation lead to the identification of Morris Black M/W/10/21/1929 as the victim. He was identified through fingerprints provided by North Charleston, SC Police.
>
> It was learned that Morris Black resided at 2213 Avenue K #1. It is believed that Robert Durst visited and/or lived at 2213 Avenue K #2.
>
> A search warrant conducted at 2213 Avenue K #1 and 2213 Avenue K #2 lead to the recovery of physical evidence that established sufficient probable cause to request a warrant for the arrest of Robert Durst for Murder. On October 9, 2001, an arrest warrant was issued with a bond of $250,000.
>
> On October 9, 2001, Robert Durst was arrested in the 1300 block of Broadway. A small quantity of marijuana and a 9 mm handgun was recovered from Durst's 1998 Honda CRV at the time of his arrest.
>
> Durst was also charged with Possession of Marijuana 2 oz with an additional bond of $50,000. Durst was released on the $300,000 bonds the same day.
>
> This morning, Durst was scheduled to appear at Justice of the Peace, Precinct 2 for a bond hearing.

Durst failed to appear in court. His bonds were revoked. The case was also presented before a Galveston County Grand Jury on October 16, 2001.

The Grand Jury indicted Durst for Murder and Bond Jumping. His bond on the murder indictment has been set at $1,000,000. His bond on the Bond Jumping indictment has been denied. The FBI has also charged Robert Durst with Unlawful Flight to Avoid Prosecution.

Durst has homes in California, New York and Connecticut. He previously resided in the Dallas area and is known to have been in New Orleans, LA since his arrest. Durst is known to use several aliases and is believed to sometime dress as a woman to avoid detection. Durst should be considered armed and dangerous.

Anyone knowing of Durst's whereabouts should contact their local police department immediately.

Galveston Police Department Criminal
Investigation Division
(409) 797-3760
(409) 797-3702

Durst ultimately was arrested January 9, 2002 in Bethlehem, Pennsylvania, where he attended college as an undergraduate student. He was caught by Colonial Regional Police in Bath, Pennsylvania, stealing a sandwich and a Band-Aid to put on a cut under his nose. A sign in the grocery where Bobby Durst was arrested read, "Shoplifters will be prosecuted to the full extent of the law."

Authorities picked up Durst after security officers at the Wegmans grocery store in Bethlehem, Pennsylvania, caught Durst on their surveillance cameras with store merchandise. Durst's identification and capture came just hours before he was scheduled to be profiled on Fox TV's "America's Most Wanted: America Fights Back."

Durst left a string of aliases in his wake. Bobby used the dead man's ID to rent a Corsica and evade capture in the weeks following the murder. Police later found $37,000 in $100 bills in the car rented by Bobby. Prior to his arrest, Bobby had been seen at an area diner wearing a woman's brown wig and a fake white mustache. Another report of bizarre behavior had Bobby arguing with himself over a beer at an area bar.

Investigators found a receipt from a New Orleans dry cleaner in Bobby's possession when he was arrested. Police also learned that Durst gave a New Orleans' telephone number while trying to lease a Dallas apartment by phone October 12. Then, a private investigator working for the Durst trust fund told police that Bobby made a telephone call from a New Orleans pay phone on October 17.

A few days later, Durst was reportedly seen at a northern California campground where he spent the night in a pup tent in the midst of a group of retired police officers. The Lazy Devil B campground is about 50 miles north of Eureka, California, near the coast. Diane Bueche owned the campground and had known Durst since 1994 when she sold him a house in Trinidad, California, about 300 miles north of San Francisco. Bueche was his next-door neighbor until Durst sold the house in 2000.

A campground manager recognized Durst from a magazine photo published October 31, 2001, on Halloween, as the man who pitched a pup tent at the campground ten days earlier, while on the lam for two-and-a-half months.

After Bobby Durst's arrest, one New York law-enforcement person told me, "He's crazy as a fox. He looks bizarre."

Bobby fought extradition to Texas after his arrest in Pennsylvania, but lost. He was extradited back to Galveston, 50 miles southeast of Houston. His January 21, 2002, appearance was his first time in a Texas courtroom. This time, he was held on $1 billion bond. His hearing came 20 years after his wife's disappearance in New York state.

A stoic Robert Durst, dressed in a gray sport coat, gray slacks, and black-and-white sneakers, stood before Judge Susan Criss. After the murder indictment was read, Durst told the judge, "I am not guilty, your honor."

The judge later rescheduled his murder trial for February 2003 to give both sides more time to prepare. In the meantime, Bobby Durst was being held in the Galveston jail in solitary confinement and allowed to take a walk around the exercise area daily and use the facility's library.

The blood trail that ran across the hall from Black's apartment led to Durst's first arrest. But it was the theft of a Band-Aid and a sandwich that ultimately brought Bobby down. Security cameras at Wegmans were focused on a man in the health and beauty aids section of the store. Cameras zoomed in on the suspect as he pocketed Band-Aids, went in to the store bathroom, exited with a Band-Aid on his face, under his nose, grabbed a newspaper, and concealed a sandwich. Once the man left the store, security moved in on him in the parking lot. The man, who had about $500 cash in his pockets, was arrested for shoplifting $9.18 in merchandise. The suspect volunteered his real name and birth date, that of "Robert Durst," but gave two different social security numbers to store security and police.

Bobby repeated over and over to Officer Dean Benner, "I can't believe how stupid I am." The officer thought he was melodramatic and told Bobby it was just a misdemeanor.

When the officer ran both social security numbers through national law enforcement databases, he learned that Robert Durst was a wanted fugitive on murder charges out of Texas.

"When were you last in Texas?" Officer Benner asked Durst.

Bobby's eyes got wide, then he said, "I want to talk to an attorney."

Gilberta Najamy traveled to Easton, Pennsylvania, to confront Bobby Durst. During his court hearing to extradite him from Pennsylvania to Texas for the Morris Black murder case, Durst's face was devoid of emotion.

After the proceeding, Najamy confronted the

accused killer, tearfully pleading with him. She said she wanted to see Bobby face to face. Tears streamed down her face as she stared at Bobby Durst, the man she believed disposed of her best friend Kathie.

"I was 95 percent sure Bobby did it," Gilberta said from her Newton, Connecticut, home. "I told myself I needed to be sure. So I thought, *Here's a good opportunity*. On his way out of the courtroom, as Bobby was being led out by deputies, I asked him, 'Tell me what you did to Kathie.' He looked me in the eye for a moment, looked down, and walked away. Then I knew that he had done it. I knew I needed to make eye contact with him to make sure I was right, that he had done it. And I was right. I know he did it."

Gilberta Najamy contended that Morris Black knew where Durst disposed of Kathie's body. Plus, Najamy believed, Black knew that something happened between Durst and Susan Berman that later caused Susan to be killed.

"Morris Black knew too much," Najamy said. "That's why he was killed."

Chapter 15

The Bobby Durst Connection

IN 1998, NEW YORK investigators reopened Kathie Durst's file after receiving new tips and fresh information on the case. The reopening of the case sent Bobby's world spiraling. He had become a prime suspect and he knew it. The investigation was moving from a missing persons case to a murder probe. Witnesses were being reinterviewed. Susan Berman was at the top of the list of people to talk to. The darker side of Bobby began to surface. He started cross-dressing, moving about and living sporadically in California, New York and Texas.

On December 11, 2000, less than two weeks before Susan was killed, Bobby married Debrah Charatan. Durst told no one about the quiet ceremony, not even his best friend Susan. Susan never liked Charatan, Gilberta Najamy said, because she had replaced Susan. "Susan was always Bobby's confidant," she said. "He stopped telling her things. Debrah replaced her in that respect." As a result, Durst didn't tell Susan—or anyone else, for that matter—about his new bride. The marriage came to light when Charatan, 44 years old at the time of Durst's arrest, arranged for Bobby's bail on the Galveston murder charge and had to provide a marriage certificate to prove her relationship to him, since it was his money she was using to post bond.

Kathie Durst's family long suspected Bobby of foul play. In 1983, the family argued in Kathie's estate proceeding that Durst's behavior "strongly suggests that [Kathie] may have been murdered and that Robert Durst is either directly responsible for her death or privy to information concerning her disappearance."

In early 2002, a death certificate was issued for Kathleen Durst, allowing her $130,000 estate to be settled. Kathleen's mother, Catherine McCormack, shared the proceeds from the estate with Bobby Durst. By agreement, approved in Manhattan Surrogate's Court, Bobby's share was to remain in escrow until the investigation of Kathleen's disappearance was concluded. After Bobby's arrest for the murder of Morris Black, Catherine McCormack went back to court to have her daughter's estate closed to keep Durst's half out of his reach.

The Berman murder case appeared to be at a standstill until 10 months after her death when Susan's friend, Robert Durst, was arrested in Galveston, Texas, and charged in another murder. Early on, it looked like the break in the case police were looking for, a possible tie-in. Still, Los Angeles detectives did not file charges or make an arrest. In fact, they still had not brought in Bobby Durst for an in-depth interview. They'd only spoken with him once on the phone.

Susan's death left one prosecutor, from out of town, looking for more answers, especially when it came to Bobby Durst.

"The timing of Susan Berman's death is extremely curious," Westchester County District Attorney Jeanine Pirro said. That's because, she said, "New York police wanted to ask Susan what she knew about a phone call that Kathleen Durst supposedly made to inform her medical school dean that she was sick and wouldn't be at school. The call was placed the day after Kathleen vanished. It was widely believed that Susan, and not Kathleen, was the caller." That, and whatever else Susan might recall, was what authorities wanted to question her about.

Susan didn't keep secrets from her friends, they said. She mostly spilled her guts during her regular marathon telephone conversations to a sundry of people. But one secret she was able to keep under wraps for nearly two decades was what she eventually broke down and confided to at least one friend. According to a report in *New York* magazine, Susan revealed that Bobby Durst had confessed to her that year that he had killed his wife. Later, Susan's friends wished they'd pressed Susan more on the issue, ferreted out the details. Maybe they could have helped her, or, at the least, advised her.

After police reopened the Kathie Durst missing persons case, they were eager to question Susan. To their dismay, before they could interview her, Susan was shot and killed in a dramatic gangland-style murder. Investigators had left her phone messages, but Susan hadn't returned the calls. Did Susan tell Bobby she was being sought for questioning? Did Bobby feel pressured?

When the Kathleen Durst investigation was reopened after being dormant for nearly two decades it was expected to be reclassified from a missing persons case to a homicide.

Gilberta Najamy, Kathie Durst's best friend at the time of her disappearance, blamed New York state authorities, in part, as well as the media, for tipping off Durst about the reinvestigation into Kathie's case.

"There was a leak that New York state police wanted to interview Susie Berman," Najamy said. "They got her killed because Bobby found out they wanted to reinterview her."

Once word got out that the case was reopened, "Susan Berman was at risk," she said. "New York state police should have protected her, or interviewed her immediately. I even gave them a map leading them straight to Susan's house. But they didn't go."

Also, Najamy blamed Bobby Durst's family for not warning both Susan Berman and Kathie Durst of Bobby's dark side. "They should have said something," she noted.

About the same time police were arriving at Susan's Benedict Canyon house the afternoon before Christmas 2000, Bobby Durst was on a plane from northern California to New York City, his attorney Dick DeGuerin said in a surprising admission. Durst owned a three-unit building at 52 Telegraph Place in San Francisco, a mere five-and-a-half hour drive to Susan's Benedict Canyon home. He also owned a house in downtown San Francisco, which he had purchased just before his marriage to Kathleen and sold just after Susan's murder.

Furthermore, in an exclusive interview from his Houston law office, Durst's attorney offered up an alibi for his client. "He was on an airplane when Susan's killing occurred," DeGuerin said. "He was on his way to New York from northern California. He has an alibi."

But that was the day, the Sunday before Christmas, that Susan's body was *found*, not the day she was murdered. The fact that Susan's door had been left open beginning in the late hours of Friday or wee hours of Saturday, which her loose dogs point to, until the police arrived Sunday afternoon makes the time of death most probably a day and a half earlier. The airplane alibi doesn't help Durst. In fact, instead of serving as proof that Durst could not have killed Susan, it places Durst squarely in California at the time of Susan's murder. Were Bobby Durst the killer, he easily could have driven the 375 miles back up the coast on Interstate 5 to northern California, returning on Saturday with time to spare to catch his plane to New York the next day, Sunday morning, just before noon.

Gilberta Najamy, raised another interesting wrinkle in Susan's murder investigation. She has questioned the duration of time between Susan's murder and notification of the public.

"The interesting thing about Susan's murder," said Najamy (who sometimes spells her name Gilberte), "is the time elapsed from when she was found and when police told the media. The time span gave Durst two weeks to construct an alibi. It didn't hit the papers until January 5th. I'm very curious about those two weeks. I think it's because of who he is. He does what he does best and that's to keep himself out of trouble. As soon as I heard Susan was murdered, I said, 'Do you think?'"

With Durst back home in New York, after flying there from California on the day Susan's body was found, gone forever was the opportunity for police to take residue tests of Durst's clothing, hands, and shoes. It was another lost opportunity for police.

Did police look in the wrong direction, at Nyle Brenner, because of his troubled friendship with Susan, instead of looking to Bobby Durst for answers? They say no. Still, they did not seek a formal interview with Bobby Durst or look at him as a serious suspect until *after* he was arrested for another murder, this one in Galveston, Texas, nearly a year after Susan's death.

At a memorial service held in early February, there was a flurry of speculation during an after-cocktail party. The memorial was held at the Writers Guild of America office in Los Angeles. Sareb had explicitly banned members of the working press who were not there as friends of Susan's, because he wanted Durst to be able to attend without being bothered by the media. Bobby, however, failed to show, just as he had missed Susan's funeral the month before. Once again, it looked as if Bobby was afraid of something to miss the funeral of a woman who was his best friend for more than three decades. He gave her away at her wedding, he gave her large sums of money, he provided moral support, but he didn't make it to both her funeral and memorial services. It didn't look good for Bobby.

At the memorial service, the first speculation among her friends arose, according to *New York* magazine, with talk of Durst and whether he'd murdered his wife Kathie and her mysterious disappearance January 1982.

Mystery writer Julie Smith was alarmed when one of Susan's friends reportedly said, "Susan used to tell me it all the time. She would say, 'Bobby did it, but that doesn't mean we don't love him. Kathie's gone. There's nothing we can do. And we love Bob.'"

The unnamed friend said he pressed Susan at the time, asking how she knew. Susan reportedly replied, "Because he told me." Susan had revealed to more than one person that she'd provided Bobby's alibi the night Kathie turned up missing, which could explain the phone call from a woman to Kathie's medical school dean. At the same time,

Susan insisted to friends, it did not mean she thought Bobby was guilty of *killing* Kathie, just that he knew what had happened to her.

Another friend of Susan's said she and Bobby had a mutual understanding to keep the secret under wraps. For 20 years, Bobby Durst apparently felt comfortable with that pact.

Conclusion

THREE PEOPLE ASSOCIATED with Bobby Durst are either dead or missing. First, his wife was missing and he told police he was the last one to see her alive. Second, Susan Berman, his good friend, was murdered. Third, Morris Black, a neighbor of Bobby's, was murdered and chopped up. Bobby has admitted to murdering Black.

Did Bobby lose it and cut down those he thought could tie him to his first wife's disappearance, namely Susan Berman and Morris Black? At face value, it's plausible. His lifetime confidant, Susan Berman, who knew him better than anyone else, is gone. Any information she may have had about Kathleen's disappearance went to the grave with her.

Though they don't say it publicly, many in law enforcement, including those in the Los Angeles Police Department, believe Bobby Durst murdered Susan Berman.

Durst's attorney, on the other hand, adamantly denies his client had anything to do with Berman's slaying.

From his jailhouse cell, Bobby Durst, too, has denied it. Durst said he had nothing to do with Susan's murder. Durst told this to Sareb Kaufman, while in jail for the murder of Black in Texas.

Authorities were hopeful that the Texas murder charge against Bobby Durst would be the break they were looking for in the disappearance of Kathie Durst and the murder of Susan Berman. They were looking for possible links. Those hopes were temporarily dashed when Durst failed to appear for a Texas bond hearing scheduled for October 16, 2001. Durst officially became a fugitive of the law, on the lam for two-and-a-half months.

Upon his arrest, Anne Marie Corbalis, a spokeswoman for the Westchester County district attorney's office, said, "It's good news because we have what we believe to be a dangerous person out of people's harm's way. We'd like to bring closure for the Kathleen Durst family. We have a missing persons case we'd like to solve."

Durst eluded police by dressing as a woman and sometimes claiming to be mute.

He was the subject of several television shows in early 2002, including ABCs "Vanished" and "Prime Time Live." And the Durst manhunt was featured on "America's Most Wanted."

Suddenly, the "Durst connection" piqued the

interest of the national media. By early February in Los Angeles, the press had invaded Susan's former Benedict Canyon neighborhood. The questions being asked by the national media were this: Was Susan killed because she'd been harboring a secret about Bobby? Was he giving her cash out of kindness, or as hush money, to buy her silence?

Just days into Susan's murder investigation, LAPD detectives expressed skepticism at a connection between the Kathie Durst missing persons case and Susan's murder. However, a month later they were working with New York Police Department detectives, looking for a possible link between the cases.

Sareb Kaufman spoke with Bobby Durst in early March 2002 through a Plexiglas barrier in the Galveston city jail. Bobby wore powder-blue jailhouse garb and was growing out the hair on his once-clean-shaven head. When Bobby was arrested a month earlier, he was bald, including his eyebrows.

Sareb went there to hear Bobby's side of the story.

"I went not knowing what to think," Sareb told *New York* magazine about his two-hour visit with Bobby. "How could I not go? This was a person my mother trusted more than anyone. I came out feeling that this was one of Susan's dearest friends, and I want to give him the benefit of the doubt."

Eighteen months after Susan Berman's death, the LAPD hadn't filed a case with the Los Angeles

County District Attorney's office for prosecution, according to Joseph Scott, a spokesman for the D.A.'s office.

In April 2002, Lieutenant Clay Farrell said officers were "still doing the Berman investigation" but that detectives assigned to the investigation had other cases to work on besides the Berman murder and hers was just one of many.

"We just keep plodding along," the lieutenant said. "The guys working the investigation have other cases. There's less activity at times. Generally speaking, it averages out to be two detectives working on it at any given time. But it varies, depending on what we're doing on the case. There's nothing imminent happening."

It was an unusual admission, that officers were moving on to other cases, with Susan's file just one in a stack of many.

Months into Susan's investigation, there were reports that Galveston Police had run ballistics tests on a gun found in Bobby Durst's car at the time of his arrest. The test was done to see whether the 9-millimeter gun found in Bobby's car was the same one used to kill Susan Berman. Police compared the gun with a bullet casing collected at the scene of Susan's murder. But police were being mum about the results. Lieutenant Farrell said this: "We're acutely aware of the gun results and ballistic results. And we are not commenting on the ballistics. It's been reported that they [Galveston police] have a 9-millimeter weapon. Their agency, not LAPD, is testing the gun. We're continuing to interview people." With his arrest for a different murder, LAPD were investigating Durst. "The circumstances surrounding Durst now, of course, mandate that we take a look at him and evaluate the circumstances surrounding his recent arrest and any other evidence or issues that may or may not pertain to Susan Berman," Farrell said. "This is a murder where there involves a crime inside of a residence, and naturally we're very reliant upon evidence at the scene and information derived from interviews with her friends and associates. We have to look at all this evidence with considerable circumspection. And we have not publicly identified any suspects. We are continuing to assess information derived from those interviews and evidence."

Detective Jerry Stevens commented to me about Bobby Durst. "Mr. Durst is just another person we're interested in talking with," the investigator said. "I can't get into the merits of the case."

An insider at LAPD said an attitude common in dual murder investigations is that detectives look at the possible perpetrator as already facing prison time for an unrelated murder. In other words, he's going to get prison time, one way or the other, and it doesn't matter for which crime. It's a lot of work putting together a case against a suspect. So why bother? Let someone in another jurisdiction put him away, the source said.

Still, Lieutenant Farrell said that Durst "certainly appears to have shown a propensity to violence. His recent criminal behavior puts a burden on us to take a look at him."

Meanwhile, Galveston police detectives were probing the murder of Morris Black, whom Bobby Durst admitted killing.

Later it was revealed that the LAPD was in possession for more than a year of a handwritten envelope police received shortly after Susan's murder. It contained a single sheet of paper with Susan's address handwritten on it and the single word *CADAVER*, also handwritten, all in caps. The writing on the envelope and letter was analyzed by an LAPD handwriting expert. Durst's attorney, Dick DeGuerin, insisted it was not his client's writing. DeGuerin, who represented the survivors and families in the Branch Davidians' wrongful-death lawsuit against the government, called any comparison similar to "reading tea leaves."

"We gave them [LAPD investigators] handwriting samples this week [the first week in May 2002]," DeGuerin said. "We asked to see what they had. They didn't want to show it. We gave them a sample anyway. What I originally told them was Mr. Durst makes no bones about having written to Susan and having given her money in the past. They corresponded back and forth. It sounds like they're trying to either tie it to him or eliminate him. Being the cynic I am, I assume they're trying to get some kind of evidence that my client wrote the note. He didn't."

"Besides," DeGuerin added, "he's got an MBA and he knows how to spell Beverly," referring to the misspelling on the envelope of the city Beverly Hills where Susan lived.

Once the envelope and letter became known, investigators still publicly insisted they had no suspects, but their legal actions showed otherwise. Investigators appeared to be closing in on Bobby Durst by requesting that a judge order Durst to undergo a handwriting analysis.

Durst's attorney also commented on what he described as "clever machinations" by the police. "They did interview Mr. Durst by telephone once, right after Susan Berman was killed," DeGuerin said. "My client has cooperated. He offered to cooperate and they finally made a formal request through the courts in Galveston for handwriting examples. We didn't oppose that. We just wanted some ground rules laid down. The judge granted most of our requests for ground rules." DeGuerin said he made himself available to police. Instead, LAPD investigators requested Durst's handwriting samples through the court system.

"Bob Durst wants to cooperate in every way that he can with the LAPD, because he doesn't have anything whatsoever to hide," DeGuerin said. "I asked to have the L.A. police contact me directly. They've never contacted me. I've been sitting here waiting for them to contact me. I have yet to receive a single call from them."

DeGuerin concurred that police had not formally named his client as a suspect in the Berman case. "He's never been told that," he said.

DeGuerin also said his office had hired "our own handwriting expert" to analyze the cadaver letter and envelope. As of April 2002, DeGuerin said he had not received a copy of the letter.

As for a connection to the Morris Black murder and Berman's, DeGuerin said, "The judge in the case has said that Susan's killing may not be mentioned during the Galveston trial. The LAPD have never contacted me, even though I offered to meet with them."

In the meantime, the investigators on the Susan Berman case, detectives Roberts and Phillips, looked to see whether the murder was mob-connected. Roberts told reporters, "We have pretty much ruled out a home-invasion robbery. It looked like she was the target, as she had nothing in the house worth stealing. She was on hard times. It looked like the target of the murder was her. A mob hit? We have to look at every angle, of course."

Bobby Durst telephoned Sareb Kaufman after the story broke about the cadaver letter and denied writing it and sending it to Susan. Like his attorney, Durst said, "It's absolutely ridiculous."

During Sareb's jailhouse visit, Bobby Durst asked how Sareb thought Susan might have reacted to Bobby's admission that he killed Morris Black.

Sareb told him, "She'd be standing by you, like she always did." It was a testament to Susan's unwavering loyalty to Bobby, no matter what.

Robert Alan Durst's trial in the murder of Morris Jack Black was set to begin Tuesday, September 9, 2002, in Galveston, Texas. It was delayed until February 2003. The judge, Susan Criss, ruled that no mention of Susan Berman's murder and no mention of Durst's missing wife Kathleen could be made during the trial, so as not to unfairly prejudice jurors. The Los Angeles Police Department and New York investigators would have to take their turns at further investigating Bobby Durst in connection with those cases and any link to the Black murder.

An unsolved murder, author and Miami crime reporter Edna Buchanan once wrote, is an unsolved story. Until the Susan Berman case is solved, her story won't be complete. Until then, a killer is out there, most probably already in jail, but still getting away with murder.

Susan Berman's Credits

Books
The Underground Guide To The College Of Your Choice, reference, 1971
Driver, Give a Soldier a Lift, paperback novel, 1976
Easy Street: The True Story of a Mob Family, hardcover memoir (reprinted in paperback, 1981)
Lady Las Vegas: The Inside Story Behind America's Neon Oasis, hardcover memoir, 1996
Fly Away Home, paperback novel, 1996
Spiderweb, paperback novel, 1997

Documentary
The Real Las Vegas, A&E four-part series, cowriter, coproducer, 1996

TV
People TV, Westinghouse "Evening Show," eight episodes, 1978

Bibliography

Berman, Susan. *Driver, Give a Soldier a Lift*. New York, New York: Putnam, 1976.

Berman, Susan. *Easy Street: The True Story of a Mob Family*. New York, New York: The Dial Press, 1981.

Berman, Susan. *Fly Away Home*. New York, New York: Avon Books, 1996.

Berman, Susan. *Lady Las Vegas: The Inside Story Behind America's Neon Oasis*. New York, New York: TV Books, 1996.

Berman, Susan. *Spiderweb*. New York, New York: Avon Books, 1997.

Cantor, Norman F. *The Jewish Experience*. New York, New York: Book Sales, 1999.

Demaris, Ovid, and Reid, Ed. *The Green Felt Jungle*. Cutchogue, New York: Buccaneer Books, 1963.

Farrell, Ronald A. *The Black Book and the Mob: The Untold Story of Control of Nevada's Casinos*. Madison, Wisconsin: University of Wisconsin Press, 1995.

Lacey, Robert. *Little Man: Meyer Lansky and the Gangster Life*. Boston, Massachusetts: Little, Brown and Co., 1991.

MacNee, Marie J. *The Crime Encyclopedia: The*

World's Most Notorious Outlaws, Mobsters and Crooks. New York, New York: The Gale Group, 1999.

Rockaway, Robert. Paperback ed., *But He Was Good to His Mother: The Lives and Crimes of Jewish Gangsters*. Jerusalem, Israel and New York, New York: Gefen, 2000.

Sifakis, Carl. *The Mafia Encyclopedia, Second Edition*. Detroit, Michigan: Checkmark Books, 1999.

Turner, Wallace. *Gambler's Money*. Boston, Massachusetts: Houghton Mifflin, 1965.